Twayne's English Authors Series

Sylvia E. Bowman, *Editor*

INDIANA UNIVERSITY

Andrew Marvell

Andrew Marvell

By LAWRENCE W. HYMAN

Brooklyn College

Twayne Publishers, Inc.   ::   New York

Preface

Although never completely forgotten since his death in 1678, Andrew Marvell has become accepted as an important and serious poet only in the twentieth century. In 1921, the tercentenary of his birth, Marvell's lyrics occupied a prominent position in Sir Herbert Grierson's famous edition of *Metaphysical Lyrics and Poems;* and his poetry was the sole subject in an equally famous review of that book by T. S. Eliot. A generation later, when metaphysical poetry became accepted as part of the main tradition of English poetry, Marvell—along with John Donne and George Herbert—became the subject of scholarly investigations. Through the work of Margoliouth, Legouis, Bradbrook, Wallerstein, Allen, and Røstvig, to name only a few, students have been shown that, subtle and individual as his poetry may be, Marvell's paradoxical wit and his urbane tone have their roots in a long tradition of Renaissance, Medieval, and Classical poetry, as well as in Christian, Platonic, and Hermetic doctrine. In short, Marvell is now a standard author whose text, contemporary references, literary antecedents, philosophical sources, and stylistic devices have been (and continue to be) the subject of extensive exegesis and interpretation. What then is the task of the next generation of scholars and critics?

Like his coy mistress, Marvell undoubtedly "deserves this State" of being considered a major writer with scholarly commentary growing "Vaster then Empires." But, as with all poets, there is a danger that the poem's "Beauty shall no more be found," that the immediacy of the impact, the passion and the wit, will be buried by the ashes and dust of exegesis and interpretation. One may argue that if scholarship does lead us away from the poem rather than bring us closer to it, the fault is in the reader. One man's barrier may be another man's bridge. But all can agree that scholarship should be presented in such a way that it serves to sharpen the impact of the poem rather than dissipate it, and to fulfill this objective will be the first aim of this book. Marvell's relationship to the literary and philosophical traditions will be discussed—often in some detail. But an effort will be made to use the general concepts and traditions to define more precisely the feelings and tones which are distinctively Marvell's. And every effort will be made to avoid using the poems as exemplifications of general concepts.

A second function of this work will be to bring together all of the lyric poems into a definite pattern centered on a fundamental conflict between action and withdrawal. There is an obvious danger in relating very different poems to such a simple polarity. Marvell undoubtedly wrote individual poems and not a spiritual autobiography. But no one who reads all of his lyric poems can help noticing the recurrence of certain themes, images, and moods. In the political poems, for example, the tendency toward action can be seen in the support of Cromwell, and the tendency toward withdrawal in his praise of Lord Fairfax. In the love poetry, the "action" takes the form of sexuality, and withdrawal the form of a praise of innocence. Both tendencies, as will be shown, come together in the best lyrics, such as "The Garden." Action and withdrawal are admittedly elastic terms. But it is hoped that this elasticity will allow the individual mood of each poem to come through; in any case, it is better to stretch the pattern than to distort the poem. (Since there is no evidence to support any order of composition, we will assume with most commentators that all the lyrics were written sometime between 1650 and 1653. But even if other dates are assumed for these poems, or if other dates are subsequently discovered, the pattern presented here would not be affected.)

The final section of the book will be devoted to Marvell's satire in prose and verse. The man who devoted himself to politics and political writing seems to be a very different one from the celebrator of nature and the critic of love. But an attempt will be made to show some connections between the two aspects of Marvell's life. The poems to Cromwell form both a chronological and a thematic bridge from lyric to satire.

Preface

Marvell's reputation is so high at the present time that there is no need either to justify his importance or to prove again his excellence. But there is a still more important reason for saying little about his comparative rank. As C. S. Lewis has noted in his stimulating *An Experiment in Criticism,* a poet's greatness or importance depends more, in the long run, on the way he is read than on what purport to be "objective" reasons for his being good or bad. Nothing is to be gained, therefore, by adding or subtracting one more voice about the merit of each poem or about the poet's relative standing. Some evaluation will necessarily be given from a number of viewpoints. The primary emphasis, however, will be on better ways of reading the poems. And by "better" is meant—again in agreement with Professor Lewis—a reading which is independent of the validity of the ideas or of sympathy with the feelings. A better reading should point to deeper meanings and to a more distinctive pattern of feeling than is usually attained by the casual reader. For in this way we can emphasize the unique quality which poetry alone gives: the ability to repeat an experience and to obtain ever-widening perspective and insight. In brief, it is hoped that this study will reveal that Marvell cannot only be read but re-read with continuing pleasure.

For what merit there may be in this book, I would like to thank Professor Marjorie H. Nicolson for her perceptive criticism of an early attempt to deal with Marvell's poetry. I am also grateful to my colleagues and friends—particularly Gladys Haase, Richard H. Barker, and Paul E. Memmo, Jr.—for reading some of this material when it first appeared in scholarly journals.

LAWRENCE W. HYMAN

Brooklyn College

Contents

Contents

Chronology

(All dates are in old style calendar.)

1621   March 31, Andrew Marvell born at Winestead rectory in Yorkshire and near Hull.

1624   His father become master of Holy Trinity Church and also of the Grammar School at Hull, which Andrew attended.

1635   Probable date of entrance into Trinity College, Cambridge.

1637   Contributed Latin and Greek verses about the death of Princess Anne, published in the *Musa Cantabrigiensis.*

1638   His mother died.

1639   Received the B.A. from Cambridge.

1640   His father died in an accidental drowning.

1642-
1646   Traveled abroad, possibly as a tutor to Edward Skinner.

1649   Published commendatory verses about Lovelace's *Lucasta* and wrote "Upon the Death of the Lord Hastings."

1650   Became a tutor to the daughter of Lord Fairfax at Appleton House.

1650   Wrote (probably in June) "An Horatian Ode upon Cromwel's Return from Ireland."

1652   Recommended by John Milton (in a letter to John Bradshaw) for a post in the Cromwell government.

1653   Became a tutor to William Dutton, a ward of Oliver Cromwell.

1655   "The First Anniversary of the Government under O. C." published.

1657   Appointed an assistant to John Thurloe, Secretary of State.

1659   Elected a member of Parliament for Hull; re-elected in 1660 and 1661; served until his death.

1660   Acted vigorously in Parliament to defend Milton from suffering as a regicide (according to Milton's nephew, Edward Phillips).

1662- Traveled to Holland; and later to Russia, Sweden, and
1664   Denmark as secretary to the Earl of Carlisle's embassy.

1667   Wrote "The Last Instructions to a Painter," which circulated in manuscript until after 1688.

1672- Published, openly, *The Rehearsall Transpros'd* and *The*
1673   *Rehearsall Transpros'd: The Second Part,* in favor of toleration for Dissenters.

1674   Dedicatory verses to *Paradise Lost.*

1675   Wrote *The Mock Speech from the Throne* (anonymous).

1676   Published another prose satire, *Mr. Smirke, or the Divine in Mode.*

1677   Published *An Account of the Growth of Popery and Arbitrary Government in England.*

1678   Published *Remarks Upon a Late Disengenuous Discourse,* in which he attacked theological concern about free will and predestination.

1678   August 18, died in London, and was buried in the Church of St. Giles-in-the-Fields.

1681   (or at the end of 1680) his *Miscellaneous Poems,* containing almost all his lyric poetry, was published by Mary Palmer, who claimed to be his widow. The best copy, which contains the three poems on Cromwell, is at the British Museum (C.59.1.8).

1689- His satiric poems were published, along with others, in
1716   *Poems on Affairs of State.*

1922   *Andrew Marvell, Tercentenary Tributes,* edited by W. H. Bagguley.

Note

The material included in chapters Three and Four appeared originally in the following articles: " 'Ideas' in Marvell's Lyric Poetry," *The History of Ideas Newsletter* (April, 1956); "Marvell's Garden," *Journal of English Literary History* (March, 1958); "Politics and Poetry in Andrew Marvell," *PMLA* (December, 1958); and "Marvell's 'Coy Mistress' and Desperate Lovers," *Modern Language Notes* (January, 1960). My thanks are due to the editors of these journals for allowing me to use material from these articles.

All quotations from the poetry are from H. M. Margoliouth's edition of *The Poems and Letters of Andrew Marvell* (Oxford University Press, 1927, 1952).

Andrew Marvell

CHAPTER 1

Love Poems

I *Nature and Emotions*

DURING the nineteenth century Andrew Marvell was admired more for his descriptions of nature than for his paradoxical wit. And it is true that the natural settings and the simple actions of the poems dealing with the mower and the meadow seem to be quite different from such poems as "To his Coy Mistress" and "The Definition of Love." Recently two perceptive critics have found that these poems "are love poems, but not in a serious sense. The lady is cruel but she is not very important. It is Nature who supplies the positive feelings and with whom the "Mower unites himself." [1] It is quite true that Nature supplies the feelings. But these feelings, although represented by such simple objects as grass and flowers, are human feelings of desire, frustration, hope and regret—and all of them arise from sexuality.

Of course, as in all good poetry, the natural images have more than a representative function; in their literal concreteness they appeal directly to our senses and stir up associations in us that go beyond any explication. This function of poetry does not, however, interfere with an explication in terms of definite correspondences to human feelings and values. In Renaissance poetry, in particular, there is no sharp distinction between the sensuous quality of the image and what one scholar has termed its "significancy." [2]

This "significancy" can be seen most easily if we begin with one of Marvell's simplest poems, "The Mower to the Glo-Worms." In it the lights given off by the glowworms (or fireflies) are compared to comets. And just as comets were believed to be connected with significant events on earth, so these smaller comets are signs of a smaller event, "the Grasses fall":

Ye Country Comets, that portend
No War, nor Princes funeral,
Shining unto no higher end
Then to presage the Grasses fall;   (4-8)

What is meant by "the Grasses fall" is made clear in the next two stanzas: the light of these glowworms, insofar as they are also "Fires," denotes the passion of the mower for Juliana, whose beauty is so great that it displaces the light of the glow-worms:

Your courteous Lights in vain you wast,
Since Juliana *here is come,*
For She my Mind hath so displac'd
That I shall never find my home.   (13-16)

Beneath the compliment to Juliana's beauty, however, is the substitution of fire for light—or of foolish passion for the truth given by the mind. Just as a wanderer lost in the night follows the "foolish Fires" of the glowworms, so the lover lost in passion follows Juliana. In doing so, he falls into sin, which is repre-sented by "the Grasses fall." As will be seen even more clearly in the other mower poems, the grass represents the flesh. The cutting down of the grass, therefore, refers to man's fall into sin. (It also has a more concrete meaning, which will be dis-cussed later.)

That the poet can tell us so much about desire, frustration, and sin in sixteen lines is a tribute to his skill. But without de-tracting from his individual talent, it cannot be denied that Marvell also made use of a certain conception of nature which he inherited. And, what is just as significant, this conception of nature was on the verge of being superseded during the poet's lifetime.

The conception of nature held by men before the scientific revolution has been described from a number of different view-points in recent years. Anthropologists, archeologists, his-torians, and scientists have, in their different ways, made us aware of what Ernst Cassirer has called a "mythic" view of the world. Only a brief description is, therefore, required be-fore relating this view of the material world to Marvell's poetry.

In our own thinking, dominated as it has been for over two

centuries by the scientific revolution, there is a sharp distinction between an objective fact such as "the grass is green" and a subjective feeling such as "the grass is a blanket protecting the earth." But before the scientific revolution there was an integration "between man's beliefs about the world in which he lives and his beliefs about the values and purposes that should direct his conduct. . . ." [3] John Dewey is referring here to the ancient and medieval world, not to the Renaissance. But a world view which has been dominant for two thousand years does not disappear very quickly. Although Copernicus, Kepler, Harvey, and Galileo had already made the discoveries which were to bring about the scientific revolution, they themselves still held to a conception of nature which was closer to the medieval than to modern view. It is not surprising, therefore, that a poet living in the middle of the seventeenth century should have seen the universe as a mirror of his own purposes and feelings.

The significance of such a view of nature for Marvell's poetry can be seen by a brief comparison with the Romantic poets. The west wind and the cloud in Shelley's well-known poems, for example, are identified with human values just as are Marvell's dewdrops and flowers. The wind is asked by Shelley to "Scatter, as from an unextinguished hearth/Ashes and sparks, my words among mankind!" and the cloud to "bring fresh showers for the thirsting flowers." But behind these comparisons is the assumption that the real nature of the wind and the clouds can be described in terms of atoms, light waves, pressure, and other "objective" qualities. Their purposes, values, and beauty are what man consciously attributes to them.

And to bring the physical properties into a direct relationship with human values—to connect the objective "truth" to "beauty"—is the great task of the poetic imagination. Wordsworth, in one of his letters to Henry Read (July 1, 1845), spoke of the "spirituality with which I have endeavoured to invest the material world, and the moral relations under which I have wished to exhibit its most ordinary appearances." Like Coleridge, he too found an "inanimate, cold world." Finding the disjunction between man and nature so great that no intellectual bridge would join them together, Wordsworth joined the two realms by faith and feeling:

And 'tis my faith that every flower
Enjoys the air it breathes.

("Lines Written in Early Spring")

To every natural form, rock, fruits, or flower,
Even the loose stones that cover the highway,
I gave a moral life: I saw them feel,
Or linked them to some feeling. . . .

. . . .

I had a world about me—'twas my own;
I made it, for it only lived to me,
And to the God who sees into the heart.

(*The Prelude*, III, 126-29, 141-43)

What was a matter of faith and feeling to Wordsworth was a belief to Marvell, in the sense that his intellect, unlike Wordsworth's, did not "Mis-shape the beauteous forms of things." As in most of the Renaissance poetry, a keen analytical wit and a magical view of nature could go together without undue strain. Even such abstract concepts as those of time and space, of the motions of the sun and the stars, and of lines and circles are filled with human values, as we shall see in such poems as "On a Drop of Dew" and "The Definition of Love." At present, however, we will return to the discussion of the pastoral poems as the simplest examples of Marvell's conception of nature as—in Ernst Cassirer's words—"impregnated with emotional qualities. Whatever is seen or felt is surrounded by a special atmosphere; an atmosphere of joy or grief, of anguish or excitement, of exultation or depression." [4]

In "The Mower against Gardens," almost everything connected with the garden represents a moral value. The artificial garden in which plants are carefully cultivated is compared unfavorably with the innocent meadow. The cultivated garden represents man after the Fall when innocent love gave way to sexuality:

Luxurious Man, to bring his Vice in use,
Did after him the World seduce;
And from the fields the Flow'rs and Plants allure,
Where Nature was most plain and pure. (1-4)

"Luxurious," as H. M. Margoliouth explains, means voluptuous or lecherous. The varicolored flowers represent the seductive artifices of women:

> *With strange perfumes he did the Roses taint.*
> *And Flow'rs themselves were taught to paint.*
> *The Tulip, white, did for complexion seek;*
> *And learn'd to interline its cheek:* (11-14)

And grafting in plants represents adultery in man:

> *No Plant now knew the Stock from which it came;*
> *He grafts upon the Wild the Tame;*
> *That the uncertain and adult'rate fruit*
> *Might put the Palate in dispute.* (23-26)

The meadows, however, like the Garden of Eden before the Fall, are innocent; they do not even depend on labor. In the "sweet Fields"

> *. . . willing Nature does to all dispence*
> *A wild and fragrant Innocence:*
> *And* Fauns *and* Faryes *do the Meadows till,*
> *More by their presence than their skill.* (33-36)

Unlike the meadows, however, the cultivated garden cannot be tilled by the mere presence of *"Fauns* and *Faryes"*; they require man's labor:

> *Their Statues polish'd by some ancient hand,*
> *May to adorn the Gardens stand:*
> *But howso'ere the Figures do excel,*
> *The* Gods *themselves with us do dwell.* (37-40)

Just as man lost the protection of God when he attempted to arrogate God's powers, so the plants, when taken from the meadows and brought into the artificial garden, lose the gods' protective power. The power passes from the *"Fauns* and *Faryes"* into the hands of man. This theme is more fully developed in succeeding poems.

But "The Mower against Gardens" is more than an example

of how natural images are used to represent human activities and values. It also introduces us to a theme which is basic to Marvell's most important poems, as well as to all of the garden poetry of the Renaissance. For the corruption which man recognizes in nature (the "unweeded garden" of Hamlet) is a result of man's first disobedience. The beauty of nature, therefore, was to the Renaissance poet not so much a source of pleasure as a constant reminder of his former state. This ambivalent attitude toward the beauty of gardens reaches its highest point in "The Garden," but it is important to remember it in the context of all the Renaissance references to gardens, from Spenser through Milton. The primal curse involved nature as well as man: "Earth felt the wound, and Nature from her seat/Sighing through all her Works gave signs of woe/That all was lost." In Marvell, particularly, this symbolic aspect of the garden helps explain both his closeness to nature and his inability to fully enjoy it.

"The Mower's Song" opens by making explicit the correspondence between the early desires felt by the lover and by his actions in the meadows where he is wielding a scythe:

> My Mind was once the true survey
> Of all these Medows fresh and gay;
> And in the greenness of the Grass
> Did see its Hopes as in a Glass;
> When Juliana came, and She
> What I do to the Grass, does to my Thoughts and Me.
> (1-6)

The poem continues by contrasting the continued fecundity of the meadows (". . . not one Blade of Grass you spy'd,/But had a Flower on either side;") with the "Sorrow" of the lover. This "Sorrow" could, of course, be the result of Juliana's coldness. Deprived of hope, the desires of the lover can be cut down like "the Grass." However, if we look at the meadows as a "true survey" of the poet's mind, it is possible to find a far more interesting interpretation. The "Blade of Grass" can easily be seen as a phallic symbol, and the lover's desires (or "Thoughts and Me") can be cut down by the consummation of sexuality as well as by its denial. If this interpretation is true, then the "fall" in the fourth stanza is both literal, concerning the grass and the man, as well as symbolic of the Fall of Man:

> *But what you in Compassion ought,*
> *Shall now by my Revenge be wrought:*
> *And Flow'rs, and Grass, and I and all,*
> *Will in one common Ruine fall.*
> *For* Juliana *comes, and She*
> *What I do to the Grass, does to my Thoughts and Me.*
>
> (19-24)

In an age when the Bible was read and quoted continually, the "Grass" would undoubtedly suggest the flesh, as in the phrase from Isaiah "All flesh is grass." Cut down by the scythe, and no more green than the poet's thoughts, the grass in the last stanza becomes the "Heraldry" by which the death of the poet's passion is proclaimed. In the seventeenth century, death (in some contexts) referred to the consummation of sexual activity. (In Shakespeare and Donne we find many examples of a play on the two kinds of "death.") Thus the death of the poet's passion, suggested by the word "Tomb" as well as by the cutting down of the grass, can be caused by the denial of Juliana or—as we have suggested as being more likely—by the consummation of sexual desire. And since death is also the wages of sin, we can see that not only passion but the poet's attitude toward it can be evoked by the simple images of scythes and grass.

A similar use of imagery is employed in "Damon the Mower." In it the lover is clearly denied the favors of Juliana, but the ambivalent attitude toward sexuality is given by the same images of cutting down the grass, or of punishing the sinful flesh. In the first stanza the natural scene corresponds to the lady as well as to the man: "Like her fair Eyes the day was fair;/But scorching like his am'rous Care." The first four stanzas then weave variations on the identity between the heat of the day and the passion of the mower: "Not *July* causeth these Extremes [of heat],/But *Juliana's* scorching beams." Since the heat of passion is sinful, we are told that although frogs and grasshoppers cannot bear the heat, the snake can: "Only the Snake, that kept within,/Now glitters in its second skin."

But the lover wishes to escape the sinful passion and asks in the fourth stanza how he may do so: "Tell me where I may pass the Fires/Of the hot day, or hot desires." No answer is given to his entreaty, but in the next stanza, and throughout the second part of the poem, the mower Damon has somehow managed to get rid of his "hot desires," and he presents himself as an innocent lover:

> How long wilt Thou, fair Shepheardess,
> Esteem me, and my Presents less?
> To thee the harmless Snake I bring,
> Disarmed of its teeth and sting. (33-36)

That the serpent "Disarmed" represents love without lust is seen also in the next stanza where the mower identifies himself with the innocence of nature: "On me the Morn her dew distills/Before her darling Daffodils." In the last two stanzas, however, the sexual aspect of his love is again presented by Marvell's favorite image of a fall "among the Grass." That grass represents the flesh is in this instance made obvious, for the grass is joined to "his own Ankle":

> While thus he threw his Elbow round,
> Depopulating all the Ground,
> And, with his whistling Sythe, does cut
> Each stroke between the Earth and Root,
> The edged Stele by careless chance
> Did into his own Ankle glance;
> And there among the Grass fell down,
> By his own Sythe, the Mower mown. (73-80)

But the wounds caused by passion are less serious than the wounds caused by denial: "Alas! said He, these hurts are slight/To those that dye by Loves despight." And he concludes the stanza and the poem by saying that only death can cure the lover:

> Whom Julianas Eyes do wound.
> 'Tis death alone that this must do:
> For Death thou art a Mower too. (86-88)

Again the graceful and extravagant compliment to the woman conceals the pun on death. Juliana, by accepting the lover, can

cure his wound in the same way as a Mower cuts the grass
(that is, by acceding to his desires): "For Death thou art a
Mower too."

The pastoral setting is also used in a very different kind of
poem, "The Nymph complaining for the death of her Faun."
Not only is the basic symbol a faun, and the speaker a woman,
but the suggestive power of the imagery and of the somewhat
complicated action brings about a different mood than the
preceding poems. However, the basic conflict between innocence and sexuality—revealed by natural images—connects it
to the mower poems, as well as to the more explicit love poetry
in the second section of this chapter.

The poem opens with the nymph expressing her grief at the
death of her faun in terms that seem unduly extravagant:

> *The wanton Troopers riding by*
> *Have shot my Faun and it will dye.*
>
> . . . .
>
> *Though they [Troopers] should wash their guilty hands*
> *In this warm life-blood, which doth part*
> *From thine, and wound me to the Heart,*
> *Yet could they not be clean: their Stain*
> *Is dy'd in such a Purple Grain.*
> *There is not such another in*
> *The World, to offer for their Sin.*   (1-2, 18-24)

The extravagance of the grief, as well as the religious imagery,
has caused readers to interpret the faun as representing something more than an inconstant lover. But, by tracing the poem
back to medieval and classical sources, Don Cameron Allen
has concluded that "The poem is not . . . about kindness to
animals, or the death of Christ, or the British Church; on the
contrary, it is a sensitive treatment of the loss of first love, a
loss augmented by a virginal sense of deprivation and unful-
fillment." [5] It would seem possible, however, to keep the poem
centered on "the loss of first love" and at the same time to
account for the religious imagery by recognizing that, to Marvell, "the loss" and "deprivation" of love are brought about by
sexuality. In the light of the other pastoral poems, therefore,
"the loss" suffered by the nymph is that of her innocence. If

the faun represents innocence, the lines quoted above would
seem less extravagant.

Such an interpretation would also explain why the "Uncon-
stant *Sylvio*" should nevertheless leave his faun with the
nymph. Sylvio leaves not only because of the attractions of
other women, but because innocent love has grown to adult
passion:

> *Unconstant* Sylvio, *when yet*
> *I had not found him counterfeit,*
> *One morning (I remember well)*
> *Ty'd in this silver Chain and Bell,*
> *Gave it to me: nay and I know*
> *What he said then; I'me sure I do.*
> *Said He, look how your Huntsman here*
> *Hath taught a Faun to hunt his* Dear.
> *But* Sylvio *soon had me beguil'd;*
> *This waxed tame, while he grew wild,*
> *And quite regardless of my Smart,*
> *Left me his Faun, but took his Heart.*   (25-36)

The "Heart," since it is compared to the "Faun"; and, since
seventeenth-century spellings were comparatively free, may
refer also to a "hart," an adult male deer. The faun (as our
"fawn") is a young deer less than one year old. Thus Sylvio
can be thought to barter the "Faun," or his innocent young
love, for his adult male "Heart." When the nymph is left to
play with the faun, therefore, the play is completely innocent;
and the garden suggests Eden before the Fall when all relations were without sin. There are flowers but no fruits in this
garden:

> *I have a Garden of my own,*
> *But so with Roses over grown,*
> *And Lillies, that you would it guess*
> *To be a little Wilderness.*
> *And all the Spring time of the year*
> *It onely loved to be there.*
> *Among the beds of Lillyes, I*
> *Have sought it oft, where it should lye;*
> *Yet could not, till it self would rise,*
> *Find it, although before mine Eyes.*

> For, in the flaxen Lillies shade,
> It like a bank of Lillies laid.
> Upon the Roses it would feed,
> Until its Lips ev'n seem'd to bleed:
> And then to me 'twould boldly trip,
> And print those Roses on my Lip.
> But all its chief delight was still
> On Roses thus its self to fill:
> And its pure virgin Limbs to fold
> In whitest sheets of Lillies cold.
> Had it liv'd long, it would have been
> Lillies without, Roses within.   (71-92)

The poem withdraws from passion—represented by Sylvio—into the continence represented by the "Faun." Strong desires and impulses, however, are not so much eradicated as they are directed into different channels. For the innocent play with the "Faun" bears a striking resemblance to a human love affair. The sexuality of the flowers is not offset by their being tamed or by their greenness. The garden is so overgrown by the fecundity of the flowers that it becomes a "Wilderness"; the redness of the "Roses" is compared to "Lips" and the whiteness of the "Lillies" to "whitest sheets" into which "virgin Limbs" are folded. (In "The Garden" the same two colors are used to suggest sexuality in women: "No white nor red was ever seen/So am'rous as this lovely green.") The tears which the nymph sheds also carry a slight suggestion of sexuality. In one of Marvell's poems, "Mourning," tears provide an "am'rous Rain" for an incontinent widow; in another, "Eyes and Tears," "Eyes swoln with weeping" are compared to the "Ladies pregnant Womb." Innocent love seems to have pleasures very much like those of sexual love. This similarity, although not developed in this poem, is an important theme in "The Garden."

The innocence represented by the faun is destroyed by "The wanton Troopers riding by." The murder of the faun by the hunters represents more fully the impossibility of preserving innocent love in a world of men. The nymph cannot "have a Garden of [her] own" free from sin any more than mankind could remain in the Garden of Eden indefinitely. The troopers have not only killed an animal; they have killed Innocence. The sexuality of the men has destroyed the innocence of youth and "There is not such another in/The World, to offer for their Sin." [6]

The particularities of the interpretations offered here need not be insisted upon; nor, as was mentioned earlier, should it be forgotten that the natural images have their own immediate effect on the reader and call up associations that are perhaps less abstract than passion, frustration, hope, or sin. What should be insisted upon, however, is that human feelings connected with passion are inherent in the images, and that to read these poems simply as descriptions of nature is to misread them.

II Courtly Poetry

It is not as easy to group the remaining love poems, for they deal with the same conflict as the preceding poems, and frequently employ the same imagery. Some division, however, needs to be made; and since the setting of many of these poems is not in the meadows, and since they use the conventions of courtly love, they will be discussed here. It will be shown, however, that Marvell *uses* the conventional forms of the court, as he does of the meadow, to express his own distinctive attitude.

In one of his shorter lyrics, "The Match," Marvell describes a setting for a perfect love affair. By making use of the same conception of nature that we have described in the mower poems, he identifies the beauty of the woman with the colors and scents of flowers. The *"Orientest* Colours" and "sweetest Perfumes" combine to create ". . . one perfect Beauty . . ./ And that was *Celia."* Alongside her the naphtha and sulphurs of burning love ". . . unite/To make one fire high:/None ever burn'd so hot, so bright;/And *Celia* that am I."

With the woman all beauty and the poet all flame we have the setting for a satisfactory love affair, as the final stanza makes clear:

> So we alone the happy rest,
> Whilst all the World is poor,
> And have within our Selves possest
> All Love's and Nature's store.   (37-40)

Throughout the poetry the woman, under one name or another, is identified with the beauty of nature; and, with varying degrees of intensity, love's flame continues to burn in the poet. Yet throughout most of these poems the two lovers do not get together: the match is never made. This in itself is not surprising; a perfect love is rare in literature. It is interesting to note, however, just what it is that is keeping the lovers apart. What is there in Marvell's attitude toward love which so effectively prevents a satisfactory love affair? No one poem can give us the answer, but an examination of a number of poems reveals the outlines of a deep-seated conflict in Marvell's attitude toward passion.

In "The Gallery" the poet complains that his mistress has "various Faces," and he gives four imaginary portraits which correspond to Clora's moods. Essentially, the four portraits describe only two moods, or two aspects of Clora's personality. On the one hand she is a designing enchantress:

> . . . *painted in the Dress*
> *Of an Inhumane Murtheress;*
> *Examining upon our Hearts*
> *Thy fertile Shop of cruel Arts:*
> *Engines more keen than ever yet*
> *Adorned Tyrants Cabinet;*
> *Of which the most tormenting are*
> *Black Eyes, red Lips, and curled Hair.* (9-16)

If Clora is merely using her charms to test them on the lover's heart, we can readily understand his hostile attitude. When, however, the lover describes Clora in a more agreeable state, his attitude becomes confused:

> *But, on the other side, th' art drawn*
> *Like to* Aurora *in the Dawn;*
> *When in the East she slumb'ring lyes,*
> *And stretches out her milky Thighs;*
> *While all the morning Quire does sing,*
> *And* Manna *falls, and Roses spring;*
> *And, at thy Feet, the wooing Doves*
> *Sit perfecting their harmless Loves.* (17-24)

The lover begins by praising her for her sensual power. But, in the second half of the stanza, the sensual implications of the sun shining on the "slumb'ring" maiden are brushed aside as Aurora is hastily placed in a pastoral scene. The "Roses," as we have seen before, represent virginity, or at least an innocent love, and are therefore appropriate for "harmless Loves." This juxtaposition of a sexual and an innocent aspect of the mistress also occurs in the fourth picture. The agreeable Clora sits "Like *Venus* in her pearly Boat." But she is an unusually calm Venus, for she is without passion. The winds and the waves, the very elements which signify tumult and strife, are calm:

> *But, against that, thou sit'st a float*
> *Like Venus in her pearly Boat.*
> *The Halcyons, calming all that's nigh,*
> *Betwixt the Air and Water fly.*
> *Or, if some rowling Wave appears,*
> *A Mass of Ambergris it bears.*
> *Nor blows more Wind than what may well*
> *Convoy the Perfume to the Smell.* (33-40)

In the final stanza whatever Venus-like qualities the mistress may have had disappear. The Clora best liked is neither an Aurora nor a Venus, but:

> *A tender Shepherdess, whose Hair*
> *Hangs loosely playing in the Air,*
> *Transplanting Flow'rs from the green Hill,*
> *To crown her Head, and Bosome fill.* (53-56)

There is still a trace of Clora's sensual beauty in the description of her hair and bosom, but the pastoral setting emphasizes her innocence. The "Flow'rs" and not the fruits are transplanted "from the green Hill,/To crown her Head, and Bosome fill."

This description of the innocent Clora is acceptable, but the reader has a right to know what happened to the sensual woman with the "Black Eyes, red Lips, and curled Hair." Why does the lover transform a Venus into a simple shepherdess? The answer to this question is the key to this group of poems. The poet wants love without any of its sexual consequences. Clora is "an Inhumane Murtheress," not because she denies him, but because of the sexuality suggested by the "Black Eyes, red Lips, and curled Hair." The fear that sexuality might destroy love and the consequent desire for a love which is free from sexuality can be seen even more clearly in the poems addressed to young girls. The beauty of the girl in "Young Love," unlike the beauty of Clora, cannot lead to lust:

> *Come little Infant, Love me now,*
> *While thine unsuspected years*
> *Clear thine aged Fathers brow*
> *From Cold Jealousie and Fears.*
>
> . . . .
>
> *Common Beauties stay fifteen;*
> *Such as yours should swifter move;*
> *Whose fair Blossoms are too green*
> *Yet for Lust, but not for Love.* (1-4; 9-12)

As in the preceding poem, the sexuality of the girl is made innocent by making the flowers "green." It is only lust which requires sexuality; pure love does not:

> *Love as much the snowy Lamb*
> *Or the wanton Kid does prize,*
> *As the lusty Bull or Ram,*
> *For his morning Sacrifice.* (13-16)

The same theme occurs in "The Picture of little T.C. in a Prospect of Flowers":

> *See with what simplicity*
> *This Nimph begins her golden daies!*
> *In the green Grass she loves to lie,*
> *And there with her fair Aspect tames*
> *The Wilder flow'rs, and gives them names:*
> *But only with the Roses playes;*
> *And them does tell*
> *What Colour best becomes them, and what Smell.* (1-8)

The poet does not forget that an innocent young girl is still potentially a woman and that the flower is the sexual part of the plant. But, just as "Wilder flow'rs" can be tamed, the sexuality which is inherent in the girl is offset by her virginity. Even such carefully cultivated flowers as roses are not completely innocent except by their association with the young girl.

This innocent love which the poet feels toward "little T.C." is then contrasted with adult passion; we can see that the lover who turns away from adult passion is one who has felt and is still capable of feeling its power:

> Oh then let me in time compound,
> And parly with those conquering Eyes;
> Ere they have try'd their force to wound,
> Ere, with their glancing wheels, they drive
> In Triumph over Hearts that strive,
> And them that yield but more despise.
> Let me be laid,
> Where I may see thy Glories from some shade. (17-24)

The final stanza again resorts to natural objects to draw the lesson of virginity, and the flower is identified with the girl by the sexuality which is inherent in both:

> But O young beauty of the Woods,
> Whom Nature courts with fruits and flow'rs,
> Gather the Flow'rs, but spare the Buds;
> Lest Flora angry at thy crime,
> To kill her Infants in their prime,
> Do quickly make th' Example Yours;
> And, ere we see,
> Nip in the blossome all our hopes and Thee. (33-40)

This linking of time with sexuality, and the desire to avoid both, can also be found by turning back to the preceding poem. We have already seen how the girl in "Young Love" symbolizes innocence. The lover is aware that this innocence is not proof against time, and there is an ingenious attempt to triumph over time in the fifth stanza, which anticipates an important theme in Marvell's poetry:

> Now then love me: time may take
> Thee before thy time away:
> Of this Need wee'l Virtue make,
> And learn Love before we may. (17-20)

There is nothing to lose in seizing the present moment. If the love is meant to be innocent, the pleasures may be enjoyed now, and so "antedated" or anticipated. But it is more likely that the youthful love is destined to evolve into adult passion. In that case the relationship is twice-blessed. It allows innocent pleasures now which could never be enjoyed in the future, and it prevents, by the enforced innocence, the sinful relationship of the future from intruding into the present.

"The Picture of little T.C. in a Prospect of Flowers" also brings together time and sexuality. As we have seen in the third stanza (quoted above), the innocent love will be destroyed by time and give way to a love which will with "glancing wheels . . . drive/In triumph over Hearts that strive." And this sexual love can only be despised. In "The Unfortunate Lover" we have the same theme:

> *Alas, how pleasant are their dayes*
> *With whom the Infant Love yet playes!*
> *Sorted by pairs, they still are seen*
> *By Fountains cool, and Shadows green.*
> *But soon these Flames do lose their light,*
> *Like Meteors of a Summers night:*
> *Nor can they to that Region climb,*
> *To make impression upon Time.*   (1-8)

It is only at the beginning that love is innocent and full of hope, that the "Shadows" are "green." When love is still an "Infant," it takes place in the "dayes." Even the flames have "light" rather than heat. But failing "To make impression upon Time," the innocent love which is "green" and "light" is transformed into lust. Then nature itself loses its order. The seas rule and "the Winds did what they please." The "light" disappears:

> *No Day he saw but that which breaks,*
> *Through frighted Clouds in forked streaks.*
> *While round the rattling Thunder hurl'd,*
> *As at the Fun'ral of the World.*   (21-24)

The flame no longer gives light; as lustful passion, it destroys the lover.

Up to this point it has not been very difficult to discern the sharp distinction the poet makes between love and lust. We have seen that, although strongly attracted by sensual beauty, the poet fears that it will lead to the destruction of true love. In an attempt to prevent this, he presents either an innocent Clora, as in "The Gallery," or the love of young girls. This distinction is not readily apparent, however, in such a poem as "Daphnis and Chloe." On the surface this seems to be a Cavalier lyric in which love is not distinguished from, but rather identified with, sexual passion. Instead of trying to avoid the sexual aspect of love, the lover seems to be seeking promiscuity.

The situation described by the poem is a conventional one. The lover, Daphnis, begins by pursuing Chloe; when his passion is denied, he threatens to leave her. But at the moment of parting Chloe relents; her indifference turns to passion. Here the conventional situation takes a new twist. For rather than enjoy his conquest, Daphnis persists in his original intention of breaking off the relationship. Instead of exulting at his triumph, he complains that it has come so late:

> *Are my Hell and Heaven Joyn'd*
> *More to torture him that dies?*
> *Could departure not suffice,*
> *But that you must then grow kind?*

> *Ah my Chloe how have I*
> *Such a wretched minute found,*
> *When thy Favours should me wound*
> *More than all thy Cruelty?*   (45-52)

(As was pointed out previously, "die" has a double meaning.) Chloe's consent is only due to grief at his parting and will give no pleasure:

> *Whilst this grief does thee disarm,*
> *All th' Enjoyment of our Love*
> *But the ravishment would prove*
> *Of a Body dead while warm.*   (73-76)

Therefore, rather than receive what he had once so ardently desired, Daphnis leaves Chloe, seeks out other women, and blames Chloe for having delayed so long:

> *But hence Virgins all beware.*
> *Last night he with* Phlogis *slept;*
> *This night for* Dorinda *kept;*
> *And but rid to take the Air.*

> *Yet he does himself excuse;*
> *Nor indeed without a Cause.*
> *For, according to the Lawes,*
> *Why did* Chloe *once refuse?*   (101-08)

Although ingenious enough, the reasons which Daphnis offers for his actions are not convincing. The argument is filled with inconsistencies. In the first place, the lover is merely begging the question when he assumes that Chloe's consent to his advance must result in a departure. Chloe's consent may be caused by the threat of departure, but why must her consent be the end, rather than the beginning of their relationship? Secondly, even if the relationship must be brief, why should that be so terrible to a cavalier lover? The promiscuous lover of Phlogis and Dorinda is not consistent with the one who gives up Chloe because their relationship falls short of perfection:

> *Gentler times for Love are ment*
> *Who for parting pleasure strain*
> *Gather Roses in the rain,*
> *Wet themselves and spoil their Sent.*

> *Farewel therefore all the fruit*
> *Which I could from Love receive:*
> *Joy will not with Sorrow weave,*
> *Nor will I this Grief pollute.*   (85-92)

The reasons Daphnis offers for his actions are weak; but the specific meanings which we have found in Marvell's nature imagery reveals a more convincing reason for the lover's unexpected departure from Chloe. If we look carefully at the images in the stanzas above, as well as at the overt meaning of the lines, we shall see that beneath the apparent cynicism of this Cavalier attitude there is the same desire for a love that is free from sexual implications.

Flowers, especially roses, as we have seen, represent the potential sexuality of a woman; and fruits (the reproductive part of the plant) represent the sexual fulfillment of love. Like the virginity of a woman, the flowers can represent innocence or, if violated (plucked), sexuality. Therefore, just as the fragrance of the rose disappears if it is gathered in the rain, so what is best or most innocent in the love of Daphnis and Chloe would be destroyed if the love resulted in a sexual relationship. The lover, therefore, must bid "Farewel" to "all the fruit" which he "could from Love receive."

The imagery in the next two stanzas also reveals this sharp distinction. Even the "Fire" the lover carries with him, despite the "Malice" of fate, is that of "Torches" which give light rather than heat. His love is not that which destroys or consumes. In contrast to the light of spirituality, the purely physical relationship succeeds with its "night" or darkness:

> *Fate I come, as dark, as sad,*
> *As thy Malice could desire;*
> *Yet bring with me all the Fire*
> *That Love in his Torches had.*
>
> . . . .
>
> *But hence Virgins all beware.*
> *Last night he with* Phlogis *slept;*
> *This night for* Dorinda *kept;*
> *And but rid to take the Air.* (93-96; 101-04)

That light represents true love and darkness passion has been pointed out in the preceding poems: In "The Unfortunate Lover" the "Flames do lose their light" when love disappears; in "The Gallery" the innocent Clora is "Like to *Aurora* in the Dawn," while the wicked Enchantress "by a Light obscure, dost rave." In the seventeenth century, the word "sad" carried the connotation of darkness, and at night even the air was harmful. Thus everything associated with the promiscuous relationship—fruit, darkness, lack of air—reveals that the lover, beneath the Cavalier cynicism, despises promiscuity. The "pleasures" must result in "parting," not for any reason given by the poem (for as we have seen, none is offered), but because of the assumption implicit in the imagery that sexuality destroys love. "Hell and Heaven" are "Joyn'd," and the "Favours" of Chloe "wound" Daphnis, because Chloe's consent brings together the "Heaven" of innocent love and the "Hell" of sexual passion. For that reason also the "Favours" of Chloe "wound/More than all [her] Cruelty."

This interpretation helps to explain why the stanza in which Daphnis boasts of his promiscuity is so forced. The Cavalier sentiments lack the ease and grace which can be found in Suckling and Carew, because Marvell is not really convinced that the relationships with Phlogis and Dorinda have any value. Only in those stanzas in which the lover turns away from sexual passion do we find, therefore, Marvell's true note. Instead of a bald statement we have images drawn from nature which express perfectly both the strength of the lover's passion and his even stronger determination to avoid it.

If it is true that innocent love must inevitably be transformed into sexual passion, the lover must either give up his search for a perfect love and be satisfied with promiscuity; or he can withdraw from passion and turn toward an ideal, innocent love. It is the latter alternative, as we have seen so far, that Marvell most frequently chooses. He turns away from a sensuous Clora to one who is an innocent "Shepherdess" (in "The Gallery"); from adult passion to young love (in the poems addressed to young girls and in "The Nymph complaining for the death of her Faun"). And even when he chooses the former alternative, Marvell cannot, as we have seen in "Daphnis and Chloe," conceal his contempt for promiscuity. He still believes that gathering "all the fruit/Which [he] could from Love receive" would destroy all joy which is inherent in that love.

This sharp separation of passion and innocence, however, results in minor poetry. It is only when the poet brings the two aspects of love together that the poems become most interesting. When the poet, in "The Picture of little T.C. in a Prospect of Flowers," realizes that the young girl who "with her fair Aspect tames/The Wilder flow'rs . . ." is the same person who will with "conquering Eyes" and "glancing wheels" "drive/In Triumph over hearts that strive," the poem reaches some degree of intensity. In "The Gallery," on the other hand, the fact that the innocent Clora, when she is compared to Aurora and Venus, also resembles the sensual, wicked, enchanting Clora, is passed over. The poet never asks how the same woman can be both an enchanting "Murtheress" and an innocent Shepherdess," or whether there is not some similarity between the pleasures of asceticism and those of sensuality. The picture of the innocent "Shepherdess" which concludes the poem is too easy a solution; by failing to take into account the sensuality as well as the innocence of woman, the poem is deprived of tension. There is a solution but no resolution.

Poetry which ignores either aspect of the problem it presents is bound to seem thin, for men rarely choose a life of action which is free from any moral questions. Nor do they, for any length of time, give themselves up to a life of pure contemplation without being strongly drawn toward action. It is not surprising, therefore, that when the element of passion is ignored in Marvell's love poetry, the lines seem not only unconvincing, but produce a bizarre effect, as in "Young Love":

> *Love as much the snowy Lamb*
> *Or the wanton Kid does prize,*
> *As the lusty Bull or Ram,*
> *For his morning Sacrifice.*   (13-16)

To one critic these lines even suggest lechery.[7] Of course, as we have tried to prove, the theme of the poem is exactly the opposite. But it would seem as if a strong feeling, when completely suppressed, will find its expression whether the poet is conscious of it or not. We have already seen the strong sexual connotations in the innocent play of the nymph and her faun: "I have a Garden of my own,/But so with Roses over grown" (71-72). Although the implications which would flow from this similarity between innocence and passion are not developed, it is this juxtaposition of the two aspects of love which gives "Young Love" the intensity that it has.

In the most successful lyrics, the same contradictory impulses of action and withdrawal, or innocence and passion are present; but, instead of being juxtaposed, they are so completely integrated that they form a richer and more original experience. Before discussing these more famous poems, it would be interesting to see the same conflict in the traditional forms of a debate between the body and the soul. These religious poems form a parallel rather than a contrast to the love poems.

[36]

CHAPTER 2

Religious Poems

THE religious poems are grouped together at the beginning
of the 1681 edition of Marvell's poetry; but, as mentioned
in the Preface of this present study, no chronological implication can be drawn from this fact. Nor is there any implication
that Marvell's religious feelings are confined to these poems.
The division and groupings are for the convenience of the
reader and the writer.

In the first poem, "A Dialogue Between the Resolved Soul,
and Created Pleasure," pleasure celebrates the sensuous beauty
of nature and the soul argues for a withdrawal from all earthly
pleasures:

> *Courage my Soul, now learn to wield*
> *The weight of thine immortal Shield.*
> *Close on thy Head thy Helmet bright.*
> *Ballance thy Sword against the Fight.*
> *See where an Army, strong as fair,*
> *With silken Banners spreads the air.*
> *Now, if thou bee'st that thing Divine,*
> *In this day's Combat let it shine:*
> *And shew that Nature wants an Art*
> *To conquer one resolved Heart.* (1-10)

The physical embodiment taken on by the "Soul" is a traditional emblem, as has been pointed out. At the same time a
sword and shield have connotations of active involvement
rather than of withdrawal. Paradoxically, it is Pleasure, in the
next stanza, which speaks of "Heavens Heir," as well as of "the
Souls of fruits and flow'rs/[which] Stand prepar'd to heighten
yours." With each side advancing into the enemy's domain, we
are prepared for a real battle, such as we see, for example, in

Milton's *Comus*. But, as the poem continues, the opponents, instead of advancing into battle, retire to their own prepared positions. The Soul in particular forgets completely that it is equipped with shield, sword, and helmet and withdraws from active conflict: "I sup above, and cannot stay/To bait so long upon the way." Its next response is even more abstract and, consequently, weaker. When asked by Pleasure to rest on "downy Pillows" made of strewn roses, the Soul replies: "My gentler Rest is on a Thought,/Conscious of doing what I ought." What the Soul ought to do is never made concrete, the battle is never really fought, and as a result the victory celebrated at the end is hollow:

> Chorus
> *Triumph, triumph, victorious Soul;*
> *The World has not one Pleasure more:*
> *The rest does lie beyond the Pole,*
> *And is thine everlasting Store.*

Margoliouth has noticed that "the contrast between the Soul and Pleasure is marked by a contrast in metres," and that the poem "passes in turn through the pleasures of the five senses." But passing from one sense to another does not in itself constitute a development of the conflict. And the regular rhythm of the lines spoken by the Soul, appropriate as it may be to its unyielding character, seems to accentuate by its monotony the platitudinous nature of the argument.

In the next poem, "A Dialogue between the Soul and Body," the two forces are not on opposite sides of the battlefield; they are locked in a combat where the attributes of the one continually nullify those of the other. The soul is "fetter'd . . . In Feet; and manacled in Hands," and

> *Here blinded with an Eye; and there*
> *Deaf with the drumming of an Ear.*
> *The Soul hung up, as 'twere, in Chains*
> *Of Nerves, and Arteries, and Veins.* (5-8)

Just as the physical powers of the Body stifle the Soul, the virtues of the Soul cause Cramp, Pestilence, and Madness in the body:

[38]

> *But Physick yet could never reach*
> *The Maladies Thou me dost teach;*
> *Whom first the Cramp of Hope does Tear:*
> *And then the Palsie Shakes of Fear.*
>
> . . . .
>
> *What but a Soul could have the wit*
> *To build me up for Sin so fit?*
> *So Architects do square and hew,*
> *Green Trees that in the Forest grew.*   (31-34; 41-44)

The conflict in this poem is thus made sharper and more interesting. Both sides advance into the enemy territory, and both
are, as a consequence, victorious and defeated. In the final
couplet the body's defeat is more pronounced. For, just as an
architect destroys the natural growth of the trees, so the soul—
by declaring the natural actions of the body to be sinful—destroys the innocence or "greenness" of the body's activities.

Since such a destructive warfare between body and soul does
not seem in keeping with the attitude of most readers (at least
in the twentieth century), it is not surprising that attempts
have been made to find a resolution in the last couplet: Bradbrook and Thomas, for example, point out that although
". . . an architect destroys the natural beauty of the green
trees, he creates a new beauty, . . . both kinds are incomplete.
It is a steady recognition and acceptance of the body and the
soul, which makes the poem so moving and so unusual for its
time." [1] The word "resolution" can of course refer to almost
any kind of conclusion in art. If we focus, however, on the
succession of images throughout the poem, it is hard to escape
the fact that the blinding of eyes, the manacling of hands, the
tearing of hope, as well as the hewing of "Green Trees," would
suggest an irreconcilable conflict rather than a resolution. An
irreconcilable conflict would not only be more in keeping with
Marvell's own time but also, as we shall see, with the rest of
his poetry.

To avoid the warfare between the soul and body, Marvell
usually resorts to an imaginary state where the physical and
the spiritual are united. This tendency reaches its highest expression in "The Garden," but it can also be seen in a less
intense form in "Bermudas." The poem is based, interestingly

enough, on actual incidents. Puritan refugees from the persecu-
tion of Archbishop Laud did land on this island, after a severe
storm at sea:

> He lands us on a grassy Stage;
> Safe from the Storms, and Prelat's rage.
> He gave us this eternal Spring,
> Which here enamells every thing;   (11-14)

Margoliouth has pointed out that Waller and others had previously commented on the unusual richness of a tropical island,
with its "eternal Spring." Marvell, however, goes further and
transforms the island into a paradisiacal garden. The physical
objects are so transformed by their religious significance that
they suggest a New World in both senses of the phrase:

> He hangs in shades the Orange bright,
> Like golden Lamps in a green Night.
> And does in the Pomgranates close,
> Jewels more rich than Ormus show's.
> He makes the Figs our mouths to meet;
> And throws the Melons at our feet.
> But Apples plants of such a price,
> No Tree could ever bear them twice.   (17-24)

When night is stripped of blackness with its connotations
of despair and sin and becomes green and innocent, we are
no longer in the Bermudas but in Eden. It is perfectly appropriate, therefore, to have "Pomgranates" enclose "Jewels," and
to see men free from labor: "He makes the Figs our mouths to
meet;/And throws the Melons at our feet." Margoliouth explains
that apples here refer to what we would call pineapples. These
"Apples" would then be different from the variety eaten by
Adam and Eve, and so they reinforce the innocence of this
garden. If temptation is not even present, virtue can be completely passive, and all sensuous objects can be free from evil.
Even the rhythm accentuates the lack of conflict, with its four
strong beats following as regularly as the strokes of the rowers:
"And all the way, to guide their Chime,/With falling Oars they
kept the Time." Neither the diction nor the syntax seems to be
forced in any way to maintain this regular rhythm.

It is undoubtedly pleasant to find a garden in the real world where fruit is offered by God instead of Satan. And the dream of a New Jerusalem was pursued by thousands of Marvell's contemporaries as they streamed into the New World. But Marvell was not to find a way of reconciling heaven and earth, the soul and the body, in specifically religious terms. His way of bringing the two together takes a more complex form, as will be seen in his "Garden." In his best religious poems, Marvell is completely aware of the serpent entwined in his apples. In "On a Drop of Dew" and "The Coronet," the purification of the soul is accomplished by a complete withdrawal from the world of the senses.

"On a Drop of Dew" is often considered a perfect poem in the sense that the theme, the immortality of the soul, is completely embodied in the image—the evaporation of the dew. We hardly need the eight lines in the middle of the poem to make the connection explicit. To be able to create such a strong effect with so much economy and ease, Marvell had to make use of certain traditional values inherent in the shape and motion of the dew. As was mentioned briefly in the first chapter, not only trees, flowers, and grass were filled with human values, but also such categories of space as lines and motion. In this tradition, which can be seen in both Plato and Aristotle, the natural state of a body is one of rest. Motion, because it is a form of change, is imperfect. "Ordinary motion up or down or in a straight line could only take place if there was something wrong—something displaced from its proper sphere." [2] Since motion and change belong to the imperfect sensible world, the drop of dew, insofar as it is part of the flower, is "Restless," "Trembling," "unsecure," and "mournful":

> See how the Orient Dew,
> Shed from the Bosom of the Morn
> Into the blowing Roses,
> Yet careless of its Mansion new;
> For the clear Region where 'twas born
> Round in its self incloses:
> And in its little Globes Extent
> Frames as it can its native Element.
> How it the purple flow'r does slight,
> Scarce touching where it lyes,

> *But gazing back upon the Skies,*
> *Shines with a mournful Light;*
> *Like its own Tear,*
> *Because so long divided from the Sphear.*
> *Restless it roules and unsecure,*
> *Trembling lest it grow impure:*
> *Till the warm Sun pitty it's Pain,*
> *And to the Skies exhale it back again.* (1-18)

The true home of the dew is not in the sensible world below but in the upper region. This upper region, being perfect, has no ordinary motion: "The skies are not liable to change, and decay, for they, with the sun, the stars, and the planets—are formed of a fifth element, which is subject to a different set of what we should call physical laws . . . it has no reason for discontent—it is fixed in its congenial place already. Only one motion is possible for it—namely circular motion—it must turn while remaining in the same place." [3]

Readers of Renaissance poetry are undoubtedly aware that circular motion and the circle itself were symbols of perfection. Therefore the drop of dew, insofar as it is part of the heavens, is not "Trembling" or "unsecure," but self-sufficient and "Round":

> *For the clear Region where 'twas born*
> *Round in its self incloses:*
> *And in its little Globes Extent*
> *Frames as it can its native Element.* (5-8)

The Christian concept of man as a compound of dust and divinity is thus transferred to the natural world; the dust is represented by the straightforward motion, and the divinity, by the motionless, self-sufficient, perfect circle. Like the long lines of an isosceles triangle, the dew and the soul converge into the circular sun and into the self-sufficient, perfect, absolute Being:

> *Such did the Manna's sacred Dew destil;*
> *White, and intire, though congeal'd and chill.*
> *Congeal'd on Earth: but does, dissolving, run*
> *Into the Glories of th' Almighty Sun.* (37-40)

The straight line of the flower and the human body and the motion which characterizes the ascent of the dew and the soul both have given way to circularity and perfect rest. Circularity is found not only in the sun but in the cyclical movement of the dew and the soul: rain, dew, evaporation—life, death, and immortality. Distinct and separate in the natural world, the evaporation of the dew and the ascent of the immortal soul are really part of one process—the desire of that which is imperfect to unite with that which is perfect.

The rhythm of the poem also suggests the movement from the sensible, imperfect world of becoming to the motionless world of being. The long periodic sentences broken into short lines and the prominent position of the numerous verbs (the most obvious is "run" in the next to last line) suggest a swift but quiet movement to a point of rest. In few poems are the meanings so completely embodied in the structure, the imagery, and the rhythm.

The poem succeeds brilliantly in identifying a human belief with a natural process, so making the "supernatural" doctrine of immortality a part of the inevitable rhythmic changes in the entire universe. But to unite the dew with the soul and to send them both to heaven, it is necessary to divorce them from the flower and the human body. That the dew (or soul) may be saved, the flower (or body) must be damned. In the poetry of George Herbert, one can find what seem like infinite variations on the theme of complete withdrawal from the natural world. But such a tendency in Marvell is expressed only in this poem, and with superb directness and elegance. It is more typical of his poetry to find Marvell as much involved with the body he wishes to sacrifice as he is with the soul he wishes to save.

The body and the soul that separated so easily in "On a Drop of Dew" are brought together in what is Marvell's most intense religious poem, "The Coronet." In it the desire to hold on to his sinful feelings is completely intertwined with his desire for expiation. The inability to pull them apart can be seen in almost every line of the poem:

> *When for the Thorns with which I long, too long,*
> *With many a piercing wound,*
> *My Saviours head have crown'd,*
> *I seek with Garlands to redress that Wrong:*   (1-4)

The ambivalent phrases serve to unite the contradictory feelings and attitudes. If we consider "long" as an adverb ("long, too long . . . have crown'd") and if we remember that Christ's crown of "Thorns" is man's sinfulness, then the poet is repenting for his sinful acts. But since the first "long" is also a verb in the present tense (as contrasted with the perfect tense of "have crown'd"), then—even at the moment of contribution—the poet longs for these sinful acts. The "piercing wound" refers to the "I" (as well as to the Saviour), and it makes the "Thorns . . . wound" the poet also. The ambivalence thus unites the material and the spiritual attitudes:

> Through every Garden, every Mead,
> I gather flow'rs (my fruits are only flow'rs)
> Dismantling all the fragrant Towers
> That once adorn'd my Shepherdesses head. (5-8)

The "flow'rs" are offerings of devotion; and, in this context, they can represent his poetry. But his poems have been used for profane purposes; they "once adorned my Shepherdesses head." Marvell could not say, as did Herbert, "Lord my first fruits present themselves to thee." Marvell's "Garlands" are profane in that his poems were originally love poems and thus connected with sexuality. But he hopes to turn this activity in another direction:

> And now when I have summ'd up all my store,
> Thinking (so I my self deceive)
> So rich a Chaplet thence to weave
> As never yet the king of Glory wore: (9-12)

The ambivalence of the phrase "never yet" presents two aspects of the flowers. As devotional poems, the "Chaplet," or wreath of flowers are of unparalleled beauty; but, as we have seen, they have been profaned—they have "never yet" been worn by the "king of Glory"—they will never be an adequate means of repentance. Faith, as well as good works, is necessary to weave the "Chaplet." But faith is more difficult to attain. Even at the moment of writing, evil is present:

> Alas I find the Serpent old
> That, twining in his speckled breast,

> *About the flow'rs disguis'd does fold,*
> *With wreaths of Fame and Interest.*   (13-16)

The "Serpent" is inextricably entwined with the "curious frame"; the poetry and the selfish desires cannot be separated. They must both be destroyed together:

> *Either his slipp'ry knots at once untie,*
> *And disintangle all his winding Snare:*
> *Or shatter too with him my curious frame:*
> *And let these wither, so that he may die,*
> *Though set with Skill and chosen out with Care.*   (20-24)

Besides referring to the wreath of flowers, the "frame" is also the human body, corrupted by "Fame and Interest." Only in the death of the body can the soul be free: Flesh and blood cannot inherit the kingdom of God. Since the head of Christ is already covered with the sins of man, the flowers cannot form a garland. God cannot "untie" the serpent's "slipp'ry knots" from the wreath; the flowers must die: "That they, while Thou on both their Spoils dost tread,/May crown thy Feet, that could not crown thy Head."

But this garland of flowers is "set with Skill and chosen out with Care." Is there no place for natural beauty in this world? Because the world and man are corrupt, must all the world's beauty and all of man's devotion also be destroyed? In the preceding poem, "On a Drop of Dew," the flower is sacrificed that the dew (or the soul) might be saved. In "The Coronet" the flower (or man) is also shattered at Christ's feet; but in this sacrifice it achieves its victory just as Christ won his victory in death: "Or shatter too with him my curious frame:/And let these wither, so that he [the Serpent] may die." It has been suggested that Christ's Passion brings together the active and the passive. Such an interpretation of the Christian symbol might well be applied to a poem in which the activity of the poet serves Christ not with its creativity, not with its weaving of "Garlands" and a "Chaplet," but by allowing itself to be destroyed. The state of grace is reached because "The Coronet" represents the active force becoming passive. As a corollary the passivity, or withdrawal from the world, is attained as a result of the activity. It is the mortification of the body, rather than its release, that brings about the resolution in this poem.

Instead of the easy rhythm and straightforward syntax which was characteristic of "On a Drop of Dew," both the imagery and the syntax of "The Coronet" are ambiguous. It has been pointed out that "the elaborate intertwining of the rhyme scheme represents both the coronet and the serpent." [4] One might go further and connect the reader's problem in getting the meaning of the poem with the difficulty, described in the poem itself, of disentangling selfish desires from the devotional. In any case, the inextricable connections between the profane and the holy, the passion of sinful man and the Passion of Christ, are felt by the reader in every line of the poem. If the mood of "On a Drop of Dew" can be compared to that serene mood which we get at the conclusion of Herbert's best poems, then "The Coronet" may be compared to some of the *Holy Sonnets* of John Donne. In this poem, as in Donne's Sonnets, the tension seems never to be completely released, despite the very logical conclusion.

The same paradox can also be seen in "Eyes and Tears," although the chief image here is similar to that of a "On a Drop of Dew." With great ingenuity the tears are shown to be the inevitable end of all life's activities. The flowing of tears represents a withdrawal from the delusions of knowledge, laughter, love, and beauty. Since knowledge depends on sight, and sight on the same organ which brings about tears, the result of knowledge is self-defeating:

> *And, since the Self-deluding Sight,*
> *In a false Angle takes each hight;*
> *These Tears which better measure all,*
> *Like wat'ry Lines and Plummets fall.*
>
> *Two Tears, which Sorrow long did weigh*
> *Within the Scales of either Eye,*
> *And then paid out in equal Poise,*
> *Are the true price of all my Joyes.* (5-12)

The tears are compared to such disparate objects as the dew of flowers, a "Teeming" moon, a "pregnant Womb," and the "liquid Chaines" of Magdalene which "flowing meet/To fetter her Redeemers feet."

Thus, like the garland of flowers in the preceding poem, the tears accomplish their purpose by action; and the active force —the eyes, which represent knowledge and desire—is transformed into the passivity of tears: "The sparkling Glance that shoots Desire,/Drench'd in these Waves, does lose its fire." The active becomes passive, the physical becomes spiritual, "Till Eyes and Tears be the same things."

The difference in tone, however, produces an entirely different effect from "The Coronet." To one reader the extravagant comparisons of the sensual and the religious recall the "lachrymose eroticism cultivated by Crashaw." [5] There is also a lack of connection in Marvell's "Eyes and Tears" between the separate stanzas. Instead of carrying through the implications of a powerful image, this poem allows each comparison to stand by itself and thus gives us an impression of light, rapid thought instead of strong feeling. In "The Coronet" the inextricable knot between the opposing desires was, as we have seen, part of the very structure of the poem. In "Eyes and Tears" we get the impression of smoothness and elegance which seems more appropriate to a complimentary love lyric than to a religious theme. Of course, it must be admitted that this poise, even amidst strong feeling, is typical of Marvell; and, if not so powerful in creating a single effect as are the two preceding poems, "Eyes and Tears" is interesting in presenting a religious theme in a cavalier mood.

We see an even more extensive attempt to bring together not only different moods but different themes in the longest of Marvell's poems, "Upon Appleton House." Dedicated to Lord Fairfax upon whose estate it was written, this poem, usually considered a political poem, will be treated as such in the appropriate chapter. So much of the imagery is religious, however, that the final third of the poem (and its most striking stanzas) can best be discussed now. The conventional religious feelings are transformed into a mystic experience that reaches its fullest development in "The Garden."

The first half of the poem deals with the history of the Fairfax family, the present Lord's retirement from the Civil War, and other matters which will be dealt with more fully in the chapter on the political poems. After comparing the garden to England and after lamenting the fact that the country is now a battlefield, the poet walks on to the meadows and finally, in Stanza LXI, takes "Sanctuary in the Wood." Professor Maren-Sofie Røstvig has interpreted every detail of this section in Christian-Hermetic traditions. The woods are treated symbolically, and the poet "becomes a lover-priest mediating between the *res creatae* and God. . . ." The statement that the poet is beginning to understand the language of birds (Stanza LXXII) therefore suggests that his contemplation is leading to a "re-establishment of man's ancient innocence and of his effortless reunion with the *res creatae*. . . ." [6]

Marvell is thus able to accomplish what he could not do in the traditional religious poems: embrace the natural world and remove himself from its corruption. He is able to do so by reading "in *Natures mystick Book*" (line 584). In Stanza LXXVI, he describes this state in terms which he will use again (or which he has used before) in "The Garden:"

> *How safe, methinks, and strong, behind*
> *These Trees have I incamp'd my Mind;*
> *Where Beauty, aiming at the Heart,*
> *Bends in some Tree its useless Dart;*

In the next stanza this withdrawal reaches its climax when, in Røstvig's words, "the lover-priest turns into a sacrifice in imitation of the Passion of Christ." [7] The stanza ends with this entreaty: "Do you, *O Brambles,* chain me too,/And courteous *Briars* nail me through."

What is particularly interesting about this oft-quoted Stanza (LXXVII) is that, when the withdrawal from the world becomes most intense, the poet is most aware of his desire to return to the world; he will break the "Silken Bondage" unless he is chained and nailed by the "*Brambles*" and "*Briars*." This circularity, activity leading to passivity and vice versa—as we have seen in "The Coronet"—is perfectly appropriate to the passion. But in "Upon Appleton House" the poet can, through Hermetic mysticism, see nature as undefiled; the world and the flesh are not completely evil. Therefore, the experience of the poet is that of a lover-priest, for the stanza suggests not only the Passion of Christ but the passion of a lover. In both cases the release from the body takes place when he is most aware of the body.

This last point is given another less mystical expression in the last section of the poem: the poet emerges from the woods (and from his mystic state) to observe the young daughter of Lord Fairfax. She is praised, obviously, for her beauty and innocence. But her destiny is, just as obviously, to be married:

> *Hence* She *with Graces more divine*
> *Supplies beyond her* Sex *the* Line;
>
> . . . .
>
> *While her* glad Parents *most rejoice,*
> *And make their* Destiny *their* Choice.
> (*Stanza LXXXXIII*)

Since this action will occur in the future, the poet is free to expatiate upon her devotion to wisdom and upon her removal from the "Tears" and "Sighs" of youthful passion. These last stanzas are graceful and clever, as perhaps they should be after the intense experience of the central section of the poem. But the fusion of contradictory impulses which is reached in a mystical state does not carry over into the real world. These stanzas are merely conventional compliments, and little more. A long poem of this kind is not typical of Marvell—at least he does not again attempt it; but the fusion of religious, natural, and sexual themes is characteristic of him, as will be seen in "The Garden."

Having reached the point in Marvell's poetic development (not necessarily chronological) where he is going beyond traditional religious symbols, it would be well to attempt a broad interpretation of his religious poems. What are the dominating ideas and moods in these poems, what kind of solution or equilibrium can one find in them, and what validity or relevance do these poems have for a contemporary reader? In the light of the interpretations presented in this study, the answers to these questions must be indirect. The religious ideas in the poems are extremely conventional. There is no idea or feeling which is original; nor is there any mention in the poems about the intense controversies concerning dogma which took place in Marvell's time. More will be said about the Puritan Revolution when we try to relate the man to his poetry.

But in interpreting the poems as such, what is most evident

is the acceptance of those basic Christian beliefs which would be common to both Puritan and Anglican. The emphasis on the complete sinfulness of the natural world might, however, be considered, historically, as more Puritan than Anglican. Pierre Legouis, for example, finds a strong Puritan feeling in "The Coronet." And a later critic, Dennis Davison, finds a Puritan emphasis throughout Marvell's poetry. It is true that antagonism to art was more characteristic of Puritan than Anglican. It should be remembered, however, that this difference is an historical accident, rather than theological. The social and economic class of those who tended to be Puritans might have had as much to do with their attitude towards art as did their theology. Despite the emphasis on the corruption of the natural world in Calvinist dogma, it must be remembered that in practice the Puritans were more apt to reform the corrupt world than to withdraw from it. The retreat to Little Gidding is one of the high points of the Anglican movement; the Puritans tried to bring about a New Jerusalem in London as well as in Massachusetts.

It was not any theological conflict which disturbed Marvell; nor is it simply a conflict between his belief in the sinfulness of the natural world and any equally strong desire to embrace its beauty. What is distinctive about his religious poems, as well as the love poems, is that the natural world is corrupt not because one is told that it is, but because the poet has been disillusioned with its beauty even in the act of enjoying it. Just why and how he has felt this way varies somewhat with the separate poems. Nowhere, however, is there a feeling that the poet would enjoy the pleasures of the senses if God would allow it; nor does the poet generally make any entreaty to God, as do Donne and Herbert, to break down his sinful nature so that he may be made pure. Even in the one poem, ("The Coronet"), where God is called upon to rid the body of sinful desires, the poet seems to be aware of the corruption which "about the flow'rs disguis'd does fold," by experiencing its fruits. Since the sensual experience is itself painful, Marvell hardly requires a commandment to withdraw from it.

Read in this way, the religious poems do not prove anything, nor do they in any way preach to the readers. They simply record the experience of a man who finds it impossible either to be satisfied with the pleasure and beauty of the natural world or to be oblivious of its attractions. The final solution, although hinted at in "Upon Appleton House," will be reserved for the discussion of "The Garden." As to the validity and relevance of the religious ideas and feelings for a contemporary reader, there is none. For, according to our interpretation, the significance of the poetry lies in the subtlety and power with which the internal struggle of the poet is revealed. We are told what the poet actually felt, not what *we* ought to feel.

To argue that the struggle being described is good or bad, religious or irreligious, is not relevant to the poetic experience. The reader, like the poet, should be concerned with understanding and responding to the different phases of the experience in the poem, not with the ideas and feelings out of which the experience is created. For example, the ideas and feelings of "Eyes and Tears" were shown to be very much the same as those entered into in "The Coronet." If we were to be concerned with the validity of the ideas rather than with the quality of the experience, the two poems would be evaluated in the same way. But, as was pointed out, the tones of the poems are quite different, and the quality of the experience was, consequently, interpreted and evaluated differently.

Conversely, entering into the experience of the poem—rather than trying to fit the poem to our own preconceptions of what is a valid religious feeling—will allow us to discover and appreciate the distinctive quality of each poem. Each reader will of course define this quality differently, but we will at least avoid the chief error of criticism: that of interpreting the poems so that they fit our ideas of what is valid. We should beware of making Marvell an Anglican or a Puritan, an ascetic or a sensualist, or whatever it is that we want him to be. Most readers are willing to appreciate the varying attitudes that are portrayed in love poems, whether we think they are "moral" or not. There is no reason why the reader cannot also allow this elasticity in his feelings while reading the religious poems.

CHAPTER 3

Three Famous Lyrics

IN the first chapter we saw how the mythic view of nature enabled Marvell to discuss human feelings and values in terms of grass, fruit, and flowers. Therefore, even when the poems were pastoral in their setting, they revealed the same conflict between innocence and passion, withdrawal and action, as did the more conventional love poems. The strong desire for love was accompanied by an equally strong fear of the sexuality that is inherent in love and which Marvell felt would eventually destroy it. Both the natural and the sexual meanings of the word "die" were often used to bring together the wages of sin and the consummation of human passion. Just as the sin would destroy life, so Marvell felt the very fulfillment of passion would bring about the destruction of the innocent love.

In the next chapter the same conflict was traced in the religious poems. The desire of the body to participate actively in the world was balanced by an equally strong impulse to withdraw the soul from the corrupt world. More success in the effort to reconcile the impulses was seen in these poems. And, in at least one poem, the ascent of the soul into heaven, completely free of the corrupt world, was made into an experience as beautiful as it was inevitable. But in an equally moving poem, "The Coronet," the body and soul were felt to be inseparable and irreconcilable. Only when immersed in a mystic garden, as in the last section of "Upon Appleton House," could the body and soul be reconciled. For, as was pointed out, the piercing of the body by *"Briars"* was transformed into a state which gave pleasure to the body while releasing the soul. This theme is developed with greater skill and intensity in "The Garden," the poem which will occupy the main section of this chapter.

But Marvell is equally well known for his attempts to carry both poles of sensibility to their separate limits. In "The Definition of Love" the mathematical imagery enables him to remove the pure soul into an abstract realm of perfection. And in "To his Coy Mistress," the momentary intensity of sexual passion is carried so far that it almost reaches its opposite—the eternality of ideal love. Although poems so well known hardly need any explication, even those to whom the poems are quite familiar will find an added interest in seeing them as a development of themes which run throughout Marvell's poetry. And in their different ways, all three poems can be read as ultimate lyrical expressions of Marvell's most deeply rooted impulses. We have no basis, of course, for assigning any chronological order to the lyric poems. But few readers have found greater power in any of Marvell's love poetry than can be found in these three.

I   *"Definition of Love"*

The "Definition of Love" is in one sense more difficult to follow than the previous love poems. The human values are expressed, not by such objects as flowers and fires—which even today carry some of their traditional associations with human feelings—but by geometrical and astronomical terms. To see the human meanings that are implicit in these geometrical forms and celestial bodies, it is necessary to turn once again to the same neo-Platonic tradition described in Chapter Two.

When Plato examined an object mathematically, he not only found that it had a certain length and shape but that it had certain values. In this living, purposive universe, the curvature of a line and the rules of geometry were not cold, abstract terms which were useful only in calculating distance. They revealed the true nature of the object. For Plato, as for Pythagoras, the true distinction between one object and another depended on the differences in their structure and their form. It was a true distinction because, unlike the color and temperature of an object, form and number were not subject to change. In *The Republic* Plato attributes to geometry the knowledge of what is eternal, as distinguished from what is sensible and perishing. Arithmetic is praised not so much for its practical uses, but "because this will be the easiest way for her [the soul] to pass from becoming to truth and being." [1] Ethical forms were thus only a higher form of mathematical forms. This aspect of Plato's philosophy was developed with great ingenuity and with even greater thoroughness by his successor Plotinus. And it is to the *Enneads* of Plotinus, as well as to the works of Plato, that we refer to make clear the ethical meanings implicit in Marvell's geometrical terms.

The Platonic and neo-Platonic belief that mathematics was a key to the essential nature of the universe persisted through the Middle Ages and was revived in the Renaissance. Marsilio Ficino's translations of Plato and Plotinus were widely read; and, by the middle of the seventeenth century numerous translations were available in English. Pythagorean and Platonic mathematical theories were revived by Giordano Bruno. Even such scientists as Copernicus and Kepler were firmly convinced that mathematical forms had human values. The circle was the perfect figure for Copernicus as well as for Aristotle. One of the reasons for his dissatisfaction with the Ptolemaic system was that the Ptolemaic universe was not a perfect circle. Kepler preferred the Copernican to the Ptolemaic universe because he felt that the sun, as the *divine* body, should be the center. In the seventeenth century no branch of mathematics was as highly developed as geometry, and in no field was geometry more important than in dealing with the heavenly bodies. As one historian of this period has said: Astronomy "was the geometry of the heavens." [2] The images that Marvell uses in this poem, therefore, are not far-fetched: they are perfectly appropriate means of reaching beyond the outward appearance of love to its eternal essence—or in his own words, of giving us *the definition of love*.

The discussion of "The Definition of Love" will be made clearer if the reader will diagram the images drawn from geometry and astronomy:

> *My Love is of a birth as rare*
> *As 'tis for object strange and high:*
> *It was begotten by despair*
> *Upon Impossibility.*   (1-4)

The lover and the "object strange and high" can be represented by two points, A and B:

A .... "object strange and high"
B .... lover

> *And yet I quickly might arrive*
> *Where my extended Soul is fixt,*
> *But Fate does Iron wedges drive,*
> *And alwaies crouds it self betwixt.* (9-12)

The "extended Soul" can be represented by a circle connecting points A and B, and the "Iron wedges" by a heavy line between A and B:

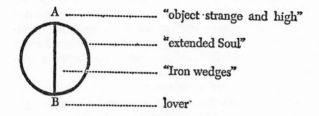

A .... "object ·strange and high"
.... "extended Soul"
.... "Iron wedges"
B .... lover·

> *And therefore her Decrees of Steel*
> *Us as the distant Poles have plac'd,*
> *(Though Loves whole World on us doth wheel)*
> *Not by themselves to be embrac'd.* (17-20)

The lovers are "distant Poles"; "Loves whole World" is the earth; "the Decrees of Steel" are the "Iron wedges," and, therefore, the axis of the earth. By extending the points, we have parallel lines:

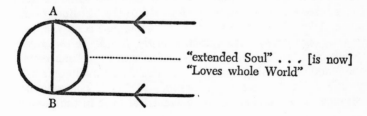

A
.... "extended Soul" . . . [is now]
"Loves whole World"
B

> *As Lines so Loves* oblique *may well*
> *Themselves in every Angle greet:*
> *But ours so truly* Paralel,
> *Though infinite can never meet.*
>
> *Therefore the Love which us doth bind.*
> *But Fate so enviously debarrs*
> *Is the Conjunction of the Mind,*
> *And Opposition of the Stars.* (25-32)

In seventeenth-century astronomy (and this is also true in the *Timaeus*), two heavenly bodies were in conjunction when they were in a line with the observer. Since the loved object and the "extended Soul" of the lover are in an identical position, they are obviously in a line to any observer. The body of the lover and the loved object, however, are—as poles of the earth (A and B in the diagram)—180° apart. True love can be attained by the soul but not by the body. We therefore have a "Conjunction of the Mind" (soul and mind can here be considered identical) and an "Opposition of the Stars."

Just as the visual image develops as logically as the geometrical theorem, so the action of the poem can almost be said to develop logically out of the first stanza:

> *My Love is of a birth as rare*
> *As 'tis for object strange and high:*
> *It was begotten by despair*
> *Upon Impossibility.* (1-4)

The word "birth" can mean "origin," since the origin is one of the elements of a definition. But the union between the abstractions in lines three and four points back and gives the word "birth" its more literal and more concrete value as well. Lines three and four also point forward to the last lines of the poem. A love born from a union of abstractions results, appropriately enough, in a "Conjunction of the Mind." In the seventeenth century, "strange," besides its meanings of "unaccountable" and "surprising," meant "coyness . . . unwillingness to accede to a request or a desire," (OED). The qualities "strange" and "rare" are given geometrical form in the parallel lines: "strange," because they never meet; "rare," because one, and only one, line can be drawn through a given point parallel to a given line. The last two stanzas are, therefore, not an isolated flash of wit but the logical culmination of all that has gone before. The brilliance of the parallel-line image has often misled readers into underestimating the force of the final stanza and into regarding "the Conjunction of the Mind" as a mere consolation prize. Actually, however, this "Conjunction of the Mind" is a higher form of the relationship given by the parallel lines. This is made explicit in Plotinus: ". . . the forward path is characteristic of body" (II.2.2) and ". . . sensation is symbolized by a line, intellection by a circle . . ." (IV.1.7.). The straight line can only become perfect when extended into a circle. "For the soul is a circle in motion, moved by its aspiration inwards" (IV.4.16).[3]

Now it must be remembered that the soul for Marvell, as for Plato and Plotinus, was extended: "And yet I quickly might arrive/Where my extended Soul is fixt." And by means of this "extended Soul" we can leave the sensible, imperfect, undefined love and reach a "Conjunction of the Mind." For, if we look at the diagram, the two lovers—the poles on which the World "doth Wheel"—are points on a circle. It is the love, then, of the "extended Soul" which is perfect: "The perfection of the circle will be the perfection of the point, it will aspire to this perfection and strive to attain it, as far as it can, through a circle" (VI.2.12). The parallel lines, stretching to infinity, are indefinite; the circle is a finite figure: "indefiniteness is the greater in the less ordered object; the less deep in good, the deeper in evil" (II.4.16).

The love represented by the parallel lines belongs to the senses or "sensation"; it is indefinite and, therefore, "the less deep in good, the deeper in evil." On the other hand, "the Conjunction of the Mind" is represented (as "intellection" should be, according to Plotinus) by a circle. This perfect figure thus represents the perfect love toward which Marvell has been striving. By extending the infinite lines into a finite circle, the poet has set limits to what is infinite, and so "defined" love. What was true of Plato's use of mathematics can be applied almost literally to this poem. It has "the power of mediating between the sensible, transient world and the world of pure being." [4]

If it is a mistake to regard "the Conjunction of the Mind" as a consolation prize, it is at least an oversimplification to regard the poem simply as a progression from the "sensation" of earthly, imperfect love to the "intellection" of a perfect, immutable love. Such an interpretation would take account only of the structure of the poem and not of its tone and mood. Although the intellectual structure is Platonic, the poet's attitude is not. Marvell finds a love which is proof against sexuality and time; but he has been able to do this only by a complete physical separation of the lovers. He does not, as in "The Gallery," ignore the sensuality of a Clora and embrace her innocence; nor does he attempt to escape the ravages of time by turning his love towards young girls. He recognizes that to give up passion he must give up his Venus entirely, not try to transform her into a calm and innocent "Shepherdess"— that to avoid lust he must give up the "snowy lamb" (*Young Love*) and the "Faun" as well as the bull and the hart. But is this sacrifice of all physical relationships, even the most innocent, too high a price to pay for the attainment of perfect love?

The answer is ambivalent. A world in which love must be completely confined to the realm of ideas, in which ". . . Decrees of Steel/Us as the distant Poles have plac'd," is not the best of all possible worlds for Marvell. In Plato the passage from sensual beauty to the idea of beauty (Beauty Absolute), from the love of one beautiful woman to the love of the idea of beauty, is accompanied by a state of exhilaration and triumph. And Plotinus has no doubt that, when we go from "sensation" to "intellection," we are moving upward toward what is best. Plato and Plotinus are also certain that nothing is lost in the ascent, that everything that is best on one level is included in the next higher level.

This feeling of exhilaration and untroubled satisfaction cannot be found in Marvell's "Conjunction of the Mind." For Marvell can envisage another world in which true love can exist in the senses, in which the lover's body "quickly might arrive/Where [his] extended Soul is fixt." This possibility was to be described a few years later in Book IV of Milton's *Para-*

dise Lost. But Marvell could only envisage—not describe—the bringing together of spiritual and physical love:

> *Unless the giddy Heaven fall,*
> *And Earth some new Convulsion tear;*
> *And, us to joyn, the World should all*
> *Be cramp'd into a* Planisphere.   (21-24)

Marvell is not satisfied with the world as he sees it, but he does not, as in the minor love poems, try to distort it to fit his heart's desire. This gives "The Definition of Love" the peculiar honesty which, despite the ingenuity of the images, has succeeded in coming through to an ever-increasing number of admirers. A love that "was begotten by despair/Upon Impossibility" cannot be wished away, overthrown, or accepted with either equanimity or grief. Both these feelings are present, but neither of them is dominant. And the tension created by this careful balance of conflicting emotions and attitudes gives the poem its inscrutable tone. The excellence of the poem is not due to a technical trick but to the honesty with which two strong and contradictory feelings have been resolved.

The sensuality which in the course of time destroys love has thus been completely conquered by a complete severance of all physical relationship. For not only is a sensual love sinful in the Christian sense, but it is impossible in the Platonic sense. It is only in the realm of ideas, for Plato, that true love is attainable: "All the forms of love . . . can only reach their true goal when they have raised the soul altogether out of time and becoming, and have united her with a beauty that is universal and absolute. . . ." [5]

II *"To his Coy Mistress"*

The Platonic progression has now been carried as far as possible; and, as we have seen, Marvell is also aware, even in this poem, of an opposite experience. Is it not possible that a pure love can be attained by the body as well as by the "extended Soul"? It is this possibility that is envisaged in the first stanza of "To his Coy Mistress." Here in this imagined world, the "giddy Heaven" has fallen, and we have eternal love, not in the realm of ideas, but in the realm of the senses:

Had we but World enough, and Time,
This coyness Lady were no crime.
We would sit down, and think which way
To walk, and pass our long Loves Day.
Thou by the Indian *Granges side*
Should'st Rubies find: I by the Tide
Of Humber *would complain. I would*
Love you ten years before the Flood:
And you should if you please refuse
Till the Conversion of the Jews.
My vegetable Love should grow
Vaster then Empires, and more slow.
An hundred years should go to praise
Thine Eyes, and on thy Forehead Gaze.
Two hundred to adore each Breast;
But thirty thousand to the rest.
An Age at least to every part,
And the last Age should show your Heart.
For Lady you deserve this State;
Nor would I love at lower rate.   (1-20)

Beneath the bantering mockery of the woman's coyness is the desire to overcome space and time: or, in the terms of the preceding poem, to crush the round earth "into a Planisphere" and to allow the two lovers who are on opposite sides of the globe to come together. Overcoming time, as well as space, the lovers have no "night," with its connotations of sin, but enjoy a "long Loves Day."

The juxtaposition of the two realms—the one eternal, ideal, and noble; the other temporal, sensuous, and ordinary—provides the basis for the sharp contrasts, the irony and "wit." It brings together the "thirty thousand" years and the woman's body, the "Conversion of the *Jews*" and the attempt to seduce the woman (the conversion to immortal life and the conversion to a momentary pleasure or "death"), the "vegetable" or lowest kind of love and "Empires," and the "State" with a "lower rate."

But such a world where the ideal and the actual, the immortal and the mortal are united is impossible. In the second section of the poem Marvell brings us back to the world of time: "But at my back I alwaies hear/Times winged Charriot hurrying near." Eternity is no longer with us as in the first section, but is ever "before us." The "winged Charriot," which can represent death (or the sun measuring time), prevents man from ever crossing the vast deserts of infinite space and infinite time. Not only passion, but even the poetry—the "ecchoing Song" which seeks to immortalize passion—is futile in the face of time. And if passion turns to ashes, the continence—exemplified by the "Honour" of a "long preserv'd Virginity"—turns to dust. The somberness, the "metaphysical shudder," in these lines places the first section in a different perspective. Beneath the fanciful images and bantering tone there is genuine regret that we cannot ". . . sit down, and think which way/To walk, and pass our long Loves Day."

Here, in the real world, eternity does not preserve the physical objects from destruction, but is associated with an unknown blankness ("Desarts") on the other side of the grave. Consequently, the physical aspects of love are seen in dissolution. The darkness that is suggested by such words as "Worms," "dust," "ashes" and "Grave's" is in sharp contrast to the brightness of the "long Loves Day" in the first section.

Why then, in the face of this horrible description of the physical world, is the poet so insistent, in the final section, on a physical union? The obvious answer is that, by means of this union, the lovers will "at once [their] Time devour." But how can the lovers "devour" time when they seem to be hastening to their own destruction "Thorough the Iron gates of Life"? One critic has attempted to solve this dilemma by linking the "Sun" in the final couplet with "Times winged Charriot"; and, he continues, ". . . although we cannot stop the chariot, we can avoid hearing its relentless succession by getting on it and going for a wild ride (like Phaeton's)." [6] Another critic describes the "sun," as "setting only to rise again," and interprets it as "the symbol of perpetual self-renewal, in contrast with human life, which sets once and forever. . . ." [7]

But these lines and the entire stanza can be understood more easily by remembering the Platonic conception that time is created by the motions of the heavenly spheres: "The Sun itselfe, which makes times. . . ."—a line from Donne's "The Anniversarie"—is a typical example of this concept. Since Marvell's lovers are making their own time, the "Ball" into which they have rolled their "Strength" and "sweetness" has now been transformed into a "Sun." For, if the heavenly spheres create time by their movements, that which moves and creates time (according to the poet's wit—if not according to logic) must be a heavenly sphere. Hence the lovers' "Ball" becomes "our Sun."

But why should "our Sun . . . run"? In some poems the answer would be obvious: the faster the sun runs, the sooner the lovers can enjoy night. In Spenser's "Epithalamion," for example, the declining sun cannot move quickly enough for the impassioned lover. Marvell's "Sun" also brings about a union of the lovers. But how different is the tone!

> Let us roll all our Strength, and all
> Our sweetness up into one Ball:
> And tear our Pleasures with rough strife,
> Thorough the Iron gates of Life.
> Thus, though we cannot make our Sun
> Stand still, yet we will make him run.   (41-46)

To go "Thorough the Iron gates" can mean to leave life as well as to enter; and, since they are "Iron gates," the first meaning is the more probable. The intensity of the physical union, therefore, leads to death—in both senses of the word. But here there is little of the ecstasy traditionally associated with a *morte raptus*. The syntax of the lines indicate that the "Strength" and "sweetness" of the lovers is not intensified by the physical union but destroyed. And the imagery—"birds of prey," "strife," and "Iron gates"—also suggests that the ecstasy which leads the lovers out of this world, into a "World enough, and Time," leads them into death. What Donne once said of the circle can be applied to the "Ball" created by the lovers: ". . . in this circle the two points meet, the womb and the grave are but one point. . . ." [8]

If the first section, along with its undercurrent of worldly cynicism, represents the longing toward an ideal, eternal love and if the second section represents love as it exists in this temporal world, then the concluding section is not a solution. It does not show us how to make "our Sun Stand still" and so achieve eternal love; nor does it teach us to be content with momentary passion. The conclusion, however, does resolve two themes. In the "Sun" which does not "Stand still," we have a recognition of "Times winged Charriot"; and, in the two lovers

who their "Time devour," we have a development of the longing and aspiration for "World enough, and Time." The ending
is a genuine resolution because it neither ignores the conditions
of existence nor does it succumb to them: "the last sentence
does but, with undiminished vigor, unfold and justify the
first." [9]

III *"The Garden"*

"The Garden," also deals with the contradictory impulses celebrated in the preceding two poems. But in it we do not feel
that they are contradictory, although the terms *action* and *withdrawal, body* and *soul,* continue to be used for purposes of
analysis. The impulses are reconciled, most obviously, by trans-
ferring the scene to an imaginary garden beyond time. Less
obviously, but more important, the reconciliation is achieved
by embodying the concepts in natural images to a greater extent than in any other poem. In "The Definition of Love," for
example, the two kinds of love are represented by different
kinds of lines and circles. But we are aware of just what these
lines and circles represent. The lines and circles, as well as the
"Tinsel Wing" of "feeble Hope," merely correspond to abstract
concepts; they do not reverberate with a life of their own. In
"The Garden," however, we see that the concepts, although
they are named ("Innocence," "Passions heat," "Solitude," etc.)
become lost, as it were, in the imagery and action. The poem
seems to reverberate with meanings far beyond the abstract
concepts which are embodied in them. It is not only the poet
but the reader who is immersed in the life of this garden. One
of John Dewey's statements about art applies particularly to
the poem: "Experience at its height . . . signifies complete
interpenetration of the self and the world of objects and
events." [10]

As we saw in "Upon Appleton House"—and to some extent
in all the pastoral poetry—the "objects and events" in gardens
and meadows are not so simple as the nineteenth-century
readers believed. In contrast to their reading of "The Garden"
as an expression of a love of nature and solitude, contemporary
critics have discovered beneath the placid surface references
which are Classical, Christian, Plotinian, and Hermetic. And
these references point to an attempt to transcend sexuality that

is very similar to the attempts we have seen in the love poems.

The attention which critics and scholars have given to this poem is enough to bewilder not only the ordinary reader but even the most sophisticated student of Renaissance poetry. Fortunately, however, it is possible to see some convergence among the different exegeses and interpretations. One scholar may see a source in the medieval poetry of contemplation and retreat, and another may see a neo-Platonic ecstasy, but there is general agreement that the poem deals with a withdrawal from sexuality into a pristine garden where man lives without a mate. An attempt will be made in this discussion to use the different sources in such a way as to make the action of the poem easier to follow. At the same time, "The Garden" will be presented as the culmination of Marvell's lyric poetry—as his most comprehensive attempt to reconcile sexuality with continence, the soul with the body, and active participation in the pleasures of this world with withdrawal into a mystical state beyond time.

On a first reading, the poem seems to be a simple description of a delightful experience. Aware of the futility of human passion and ambition, the poet forsakes human society for the "repose," and "Innocence," and "Beauty" which he finds in nature. But, if we look at the poem more carefully, we find that the "Innocence" of the garden is "delicious," and provides pleasures which, particularly in the fifth stanza, are very much akin to sexual experience. Since we can see that this garden is the Garden of Eden, there is no difficulty in understanding why it is beautiful, restful, and innocent.

But some exploration is needed to make clear just why passionate pleasures can be enjoyed among trees, or why the plants are sexual and man is not. An early attempt at an explanation was made by William Empson, who argued that women are no longer interesting to the poet "because nature is more beautiful." [11] It is tempting to accept a simple explanation, especially since the poem itself tries to reduce human experience to simple terms. But, if women are no longer interesting, we would still have to account for the fact that the beauty and sexuality of women are attributed to nature; or, to put it another way, why and in what way is "nature more beautiful" than women?

The key to this difficulty lies in the tradition, which Marvell uses, that Adam before the Fall was androgynous, containing both sexes within himself. Ruth Wallerstein first found this tradition in an old Rabbinic legend.[12] More recently Maren-Sofie Røstvig has traced the androgynous Adam to the Hermetic tradition. Lord Fairfax, on whose estate Marvell (presumably) wrote this poem, was engaged in writing a commentary on a translation of Hermetic writings. And some sentences from Fairfax's works relate quite specifically to "The Garden": ". . . 'being male and female, in the same body as the Scriptures said of the first man before he sined & before God took the woman out of the side of man.' . . . During this period they were tied in a certain bond or knot which in the words of Fairfax, 'held all things from action, poyse or motion.'"[13] But, whatever the source, the idea of Adam as androgynous clarifies the central paradox of the poem.

In the first stanza, we enter into this garden by a conventional symbol. The wreath of laurel ("Bayes"), which represents the result of men's efforts, is taken literally; that is, it is discussed not only as a symbol of human ambition, but as a natural plant:

> *How vainly men themselves amaze*
> *To win the Palm, the Oke, or Bayes;*
> *And their uncessant Labours see*
> *Crown'd from some single Herb or Tree.*
> *Whose short and narrow verged Shade*
> *Does prudently their Toyles upbraid;* (1-6)

Representing the Garden of Eden before Eve, the plants serve as a reminder of the happy state from which man has fallen. Now, after the Fall, man is cursed with labor by the sweat of his brow, with sinful sexuality, and with death. The plants which symbolize fame and triumph cannot protect man's brow from the sun; they can only fade and die, reminding him of the futility of both his labor and his fame. Man's sexuality is then contrasted with his former state of innocence by a reference to the procreation of plants. Containing both the pistil and stamen within themselves, the flowers and trees, like androgynous Adam, unite or "close"—not in sexual passion—but "To weave the Garlands of repose."

[65]

In the next six stanzas we are free of sexual passion, labor, and mortality—the consequences of the creation of Eve:

> Fair quiet, have I found thee here,
> And Innocence thy Sister dear!
> Mistaken long, I sought you then
> In busie Companies of Men.
> Your sacred Plants, if here below,
> Only among the Plants will grow.   (9-14)

Among men the "sacred Plants" of fame and triumph ("the Palm, the Oke, or Bayes") will pass away into oblivion. "Fame is no plant that grows on mortal soil." But, if these "sacred Plants" ever existed "here below," they were in the Garden of Eden, or in this garden which Marvell makes into an Eden. Fame "will grow" because there is no death; and "Innocence," because Adam contained both sexes within himself, precludes evil.

Ignorant of the state of innocence and of the evils of sexuality, the lovers who "Cut in these Trees their Mistress name" do not realize that their pleasures are inferior to those of the androgynous Adam who walked about giving the trees only their own names: ". . . whatsoever Adam called every living creature, that was the name thereof" (Genesis 2:19). In the fourth and fifth stanzas, Marvell insists not only that the garden can represent the freedom from sexuality, labor, and death which existed in Eden, but that this androgynous Adam, walking among the trees, enjoyed all the pleasures of sexuality. This is first proved by reference to the Greek myths, which, in the seventeenth century, were commonly regarded as pagan versions of Biblical records:

> When we have run our Passions heat,
> Love hither makes his best retreat.
> The Gods, that mortal Beauty chase,
> Still in a Tree did end their race.
> Apollo hunted Daphne so,
> Only that She might Laurel grow.
> And Pan did after Syrinx speed,
> Not as a Nymph, but for a Reed.   (25-32)

By the use of such terms as "heat," "chase," and "race," the chasing of Daphne and Syrinx is made to resemble a race. What would seem like a defeat is turned into a victory. The "Reed" and the "Laurel" which represent defeat for the lovers are "the Palm, the Oke, or Bayes" which represent victory for the runners. Marvell thus twists the legends around to fit his argument. Apollo and Pan, recognizing the superiority of the passion enjoyed by the androgynous Adam, embrace the laurel and the reed. Even when they seem to pursue the nymphs, they do so only in an attempt to reach this state of innocent sexuality: "*Apollo* hunted *Daphne* so/Only that She might Laurel grow."

Marvell is also doing something else in this stanza. If Daphne turns into laurel, then the laurel becomes more and more like Daphne. That is, the pleasures which the androgynous Adam enjoyed, although at all times perfectly innocent, seem to resemble the sexual pleasures of mortal man. So far the solitude has been "delicious" and the "lovely green" has been "am'rous." But after the laurel and the reed have been identified with Daphne and Syrinx, the poet can go even further; he can present a scene in which the innocent pleasures enjoyed before the advent of Eve seem to be very much like those enjoyed with her:

> *What wond'rous Life is this I lead!*
> *Ripe Apples drop about my head;*
> *The Luscious Clusters of the Vine*
> *Upon my Mouth do crush their Wine;*
> *The Nectaren, and curious Peach,*
> *Into my hands themselves do reach;*
> *Stumbling on Melons, as I pass,*
> *Insnar'd with Flow'rs, I fall on Grass.*   (33-40)

Nowhere in Marvell has ambivalence been used with greater subtlety and effectiveness. The scene is primarily a description of the Garden of Eden before Eve. It also describes the same garden after the Fall. And thirdly, it shows the superiority of the first scene over the second without any explicit statement.

That this is the garden after the Fall can easily be seen if we recognize the sexual connotations of the imagery. (The use of fruits and flowers as sexual symbols has been pointed out by numerous critics, including William Empson and Milton Klonsky.) In this context all the sensuous pleasures are evil. The "Grass," as we have mentioned in a previous chapter, is the flesh. When he stumbles "on Melons" (which is the Greek for apples), is "Insnar'd with Flow'rs," and falls "on Grass," he is falling into carnal sin.

But we have said that this is primarily a description of "that happy Garden-state." This is where love has made "his best retreat," where Daphne has turned into a plant. Therefore the consequences of the Fall—sinful sexuality, labor, and death—should be absent. In this context the fruits are not the forbidden ones but those given man to enjoy for food and meat without labor or effort: "The Nectaren, and curious Peach/Into my hands themselves do reach."

This pristine Adam is completely passive. In this innocent state, his being "Insnar'd with Flow'rs" and falling "on Grass" should be taken literally. The "fall on Grass" is not a descent into hell, but an innocent, sensuous, altogether pleasant experience. Since Adam is not without sex, but contains both sexes within himself, the sexual connotations of the images are still present, but they are now perfectly innocent. Daphne has turned into a laurel. Instead of the sinful sexuality which was to come with Eve, the fruits represent the sexuality which the androgynous Adam enjoyed in the garden. We now see that the sexual connotations are used only to show the *superiority* of the innocent pleasures. In the plants Marvell has found a symbol for passion with all of its pleasures and none of its pains. It is indeed a "wond'rous Life."

Having shown that Apollo desired Daphne only as a laurel, that true passion is really enjoyed among the green plants, Marvell now attempts to transform sensible passion into Platonic ideas. In an age when Plato was the divine philosopher, when ancient philosophy (like the myths of Apollo and Daphne) was thought of not as conflicting with Christianity but as a pagan anticipation of Christian truth, it is not surprising that Platonic ideas are used as a philosophical counterpart of the Garden of Eden.[14]

In the Plotinian cosmology, the World Soul extends throughout the entire universe, even to the vegetative and generative forces in nature and man. So far, according to this cosmology, the poem has taken place in the lowest parts of the World Soul. But above this World Soul is the Mind, or Intellectual Principle. Only "The better part of the soul . . . is winged for the Intellectual act" (*Enneads*, II,34.). The lower orders of existence, such as the plants, can attain pleasure; but happiness, since it requires reason, can only be found in the mind:

> *Mean while the Mind, from pleasure less,*
> *Withdraws into its happiness:*
> *The Mind, that Ocean where each kind*
> *Does streight its own resemblance find;* (41-44)

In Plato, for every class of objects there is an Idea of that object. These Ideas, since they are not dependent on any one mind, may be said to exist in a Universal Mind. Therefore, like the sea, which in medieval legend contained replicas of all the plants and animals which could be found on earth, the mind contains an idea of "each kind" or class of earthly objects. But once those sensible objects get into the mind, they are no longer sensible objects but ideas, or thoughts. Plato's lover, "contemplating the vast sea of beauty . . . will create many fair and noble thoughts and notions in the boundless love of wisdom" (*Symposium*, 210.):

> *Yet it creates, transcending these,*
> *Far other Worlds, and other Seas;*
> *Annihilating all that's made*
> *To a green Thought in a green Shade.* (45-48)

This transformation of a sensible object into a thought is also in accordance with neo-Platonic philosophy. It is only in the world of becoming that there is a difference between the process of thinking and that which is thought. In immaterial objects, however, according to Plotinus, "the knowledge is identical with the thing, the immaterial thing being an intellectual object is also a thought." [15]

Having become a thought, freed from any connection with the senses, "all that's made" in this world—including passionate desire—becomes good, innocent, or "green." The "Shade," for the seventeenth century, was the soul or spirit after it was freed from the body; and it is, therefore, also innocent. Human passion, which in the Garden of Eden was exemplified by a green plant, becomes in this Platonic "Mind" a "green Thought in a green Shade."

But Marvell uses these Platonic and neo-Platonic concepts to express a very un-Platonic attitude. In Plotinus, to achieve "its proper act and End. . . . The Final Disengagement," the soul "must hold itself above all passions and affections." "The Soul leaves the natural world and busies itself elsewhere" (I,2.5). But since we are in the Garden of Eden, the soul can disengage itself here below, in the innocent vegetative order.

In the *Phaedrus* the soul—which has only been recently separated from the divine world of true being, "in our state of innocence before we had any experience of evils to come"— becomes winged for a higher flight:

> *There like a Bird it sits, and sings,*
> *Then whets, and combs its silver Wings;*
> *And, till prepar'd for longer flight,*
> *Waves in its Plumes the various Light.*   (53-56)

The "various Light" recalls the lights in Genesis which measure time: "And God said, Let there be lights in the firmament of heaven to divide the day from the night; and let them be for signs, and for seasons, and for days, and years" (1:14). Since there is no death in this state of innocence, or even labor, the soul is not afraid of time. The lights which "divide the day from the night" which are "for signs, and for seasons, and for days, and years," do not mark the soul's journey toward death. The natural garden, transformed into an ideal garden, is eternal; and the soul, oblivious of time, "Waves in its Plumes the various Light."

But all this took place before God had found a "helpmeet" for Adam. And in the next stanza we are reminded that this state of innocence has passed:

> *Such was that happy Garden-state,*
> *While Man there walk'd without a Mate:*
> *After a Place so pure, and sweet,*
> *What other Help could yet be meet!*   (57-60)

It was "beyond a Mortal's share" to live alone and contain two sexes in one body:

> *But 'twas beyond a Mortal's share*
> *To wander solitary there:*
> *Two Paradises 'twere in one*
> *To live in Paradise alone.* (61-64)

The poem now comes into a clearer perspective. The garden is the Garden of Innocence; it is the place where man "walk'd without a Mate." But the poet who is looking at it, although he can *imagine* himself to be the innocent Adam, *knows* all along that he is the fallen Adam. Because he is both Adams, he can make "The Garden" a microcosm of the sinful world as well as a symbol of Eden. That is why the laurel in the first stanza can represent both the "green" innocent plants and the futility of human fame and why the fruits in the fifth stanza represent both innocence and sexuality.

Although in the final stanza Marvell again describes the innocence that preceded the Fall, it is innocence as seen by a poet who is entirely aware of the consequences of that Fall:

> *How well the skillful Gardner drew*
> *Of flow'rs and herbes this Dial new;*
> *Where from above the milder Sun*
> *Does through a fragrant Zodiack run;*
> *And, as it works, th' industrious Bee*
> *Computes its time as well as we.* (65-70)

Again this scene, like the entire poem, can be read as a simple description of perfect innocence and peace. But, the perfect state makes us recognize the fallen state also. The "industrious Bee" recalls the "uncessant Labours" of men in the first stanza; and the sundial, fragrant though it may be, measures the path of the sun which reminds us of the "short and narrow verged Shade." The garden is the natural garden of fallen man as well as Eden. The ecstatic moment has passed, the soul has returned to the body, but neither the poet nor the garden is quite the same after such an experience: "How could such sweet and wholsome Hours/Be reckon'd but with herbs and flow'rs!" We are outside of time and within time, participating in the world before us and withdrawing into complete passivity—all at the same time. It is, in every sense of the word, a "wond'rous Life."

As in all good poetry, the poem tries to create in the minds of the reader the effect that it describes. Vivid images and simple actions, or rather lack of action, create the effect of simplicity which is part of the pristine state being described. The passivity is further emphasized by the slow, regular rhythm, in contrast to the rapid, headlong pace of "To his Coy Mistress." (It is hard to believe that the meter and the rhyme scheme are the same in both poems, so strong are the contrasts that Marvell has made in rhythm and diction.) At the same time the depth of meaning in every stanza and the many references to philosophy and legend involve us in the contemplative activity which balances the passivity of the body. Our minds do not have to move quickly, as they do in the love poems; but, as befitting the activity of contemplation, we have to allow the images to sink in slowly, allowing them to act on our unconscious. They may be compared to those images which Yeats describes in "Byzantium": "images that yet/Fresh images beget."

The penetrating and suggestive quality of the images gives the poem its distinctive tone, and, ultimately, it is this quality that accounts for the poem being considered one of the great lyrics in English literature. The complex intellectual and mythical strands would not make the poem what it is if Marvell had only translated these concepts into concrete images. As we have tried to show, conventional ideas and feelings may have gone *into* the poem, and scholars can, at least in theory, identify them all. But—and this point is one that is easily forgotten—we can never, even theoretically, identify completely what comes *out* of the poem. Not only does the poem create a pattern which is distinctive and therefore different from its sources, but it creates in the reader an ever-changing series of responses. This ability of any fully created work of art to have its own life explains, to some extent, why constant reinterpretations of certain literary works occur. Scholars and critics can tell us what went into the poem and what effect the poem has on them. And these are both important functions. But if he reads the poem often, a reader cannot prevent the images, rhythm, and the pattern from creating responses within him that go beyond any philosophic concepts.

CHAPTER 4

Politics and Poetry

THE conflict between action and withdrawal, between the world of sensory experience and the ideal world of contemplation, can also be found in Marvell's political poems. Instead of an ideal love which is in danger of being destroyed by the actions of a corrupt body, Marvell holds on to an ideal of political justice and order which, he comes to realize, is unattainable in the actual world of political conflict. Again, as in the previous poems, we shall see that the attempt to bring together these opposite poles of the ideal and of the actual results in his best poetry. But the differences between the political poems and the others are equally significant.

Since a great deal is known about Marvell's political career, and almost nothing about his personal life, it is inevitable that these poems will be related to his life in a way that the love poems are not. But apart from this biographical accident, it is inevitable that political poetry would have to be read somewhat differently. For a political poem cannot, in one sense, be as autonomous as a love poem. The writing of a love poem has no necessary connection with the poet's attitude towards a particular woman; we enjoy "To his Coy Mistress," for example, without any reference to any woman or to any emotion that the poet felt in actual life. The poem does not find its completion in any action or fact outside of itself. This autonomy is also true of a religious lyric such as "The Coronet." We neither know nor need to know whether the poet actually destroyed or felt like destroying his poetry. To write a love poem or a religious poem is not equivalent to writing a love letter to an actual woman or to performing a religious or sacrilegious act. For the poems, if they are good and not occasional verse, are complete experiences in themselves.

To write a political poem about a public event is a different matter. Such a poem is equivalent to signing a petition or to speaking in public about the event. A political poem thus involves a practical as well as a contemplative act. Since there is an inherent contradiction in these two activities (similar to writing a love *poem* that is at the same time a love *letter*), it is not surprising to find so few successful political poems. William Butler Yeats, whose political poetry is in some ways comparable to Marvell's, dealt with this contradiction in his famous statement that "We make out of the quarrel with others, *rhetoric*, but of the quarrel with ourselves, poetry." [1] To Yeats, poetry came out of the deeply rooted conflicts within the poet. He distrusted poetry which presented a clear-cut argument.

If, as we have suggested, a political poem attempts to combine our "quarrel with others" with the "quarrel with ourselves," it is not surprising that so few political poems succeed in being both great arguments and great lyrics. Before examining Marvell's one undisputed success, "An Horatian Ode upon Cromwel's Return from Ireland," some mention should be made of the occasional verse written during the same period. In these poems the "quarrel with others" is paramount, and we can also see that his political position at this time was unequivocally Royalist.

I *Occasional Verse*

The earliest reference to the political situation occurs in the verses "To his Noble Friend Mr. Richard Lovelace, upon his Poems," which appeared in the volume of Lovelace's *Lucasta* (1649). Although the conventional compliments to Lovelace's poetry are made, the main theme running through the twenty-five couplets is an attack on the Puritans. Lovelace is praised not so much for his poetry as for being an exemplar of that aristocratic grace which was overthrown with the downfall of Charles I:

> *Our times are much degenerate from those*
> *Which your sweet Muse which your fair Fortune chose,*
> *And as complexions alter with the Climes,*
> *Our wits have drawne th' infection of our times.*

[74]

> *That candid Age no other way could tell*
> *To be ingenious, but by speaking well.*
>
> . . . .
>
> *These vertues now are banisht out of Towne,*
> *Our Civill Wars have lost the Civicke crowne.*
> *(1-6, 11-12)*

There is no certainty that Marvell wrote "An Elegy upon the Death of My Lord Francis Villiers," and the standard editions include it with some reservation. But if Marvell did write it we have still another indication of his strong Royalist feelings. Francis Villiers died in 1649 while fighting for the King, and the verses praise the heroism of the man and the justice of his cause with little reservation—and even less skill. Mention might also be made at this point of another occasional poem, "Upon the Death of the Lord Hastings," also written in 1649. While praised by one scholar as a fusion of classical and Christian images,[2] the poem is of little interest for the reader who is looking for a distinctive poetic experience. One couplet is pertinent, however, as revealing in a small way Marvell's politics: "Therefore the *Democratik* Stars did rise,/And all that Worth from hence did *Ostracize*" (25-26).

The last poem in this group, and the clearest expression (as well as the last) of Marvell's Royalist beliefs, is "Tom May's Death." Written at the end of 1650, and almost certainly after "An Horatian Ode," this poem bitterly attacks Tom May for doing what Marvell himself had just done—giving up the Royalist cause and supporting Fairfax, Cromwell, and the Independent party. A poet, translator, and historian, May had once been a loyal supporter of Charles I. Marvell's attack on him is based mainly on the charge that May had prostituted his art in order to join the victorious party. Nowhere is Marvell so consistently savage in his satire. The scene is Elysium, where May's spirit is refused admittance by Ben Jonson who castigates him as a "Most servil' wit, and Mercenary Pen" (40). Then in the most powerful section of the poem, the rhetoric gives way to genuine poetry. At a time when the forces of evil seem most triumphant and when little can be done in the actual world to stop the progress of the revolution, then, Marvell insists, is the time for the contemplative man, the poet, to maintain the ideal principles. If the ideal cannot be actualized and if Charles' head cannot be restored, the "knowledge" of what is right should at least be made known in art:

> When the Sword glitters ore the Judges head,
> And fear has Coward Churchmen silenced,
> Then is the Poets time, 'tis then he drawes,
> And single fights forsaken Vertues cause,
> He, when the wheel of Empire, whirleth back,
> And though the World's disjointed Axel crack,
> Sings still of ancient Rights and better Times,
> Seeks wretched good, arraigns successful Crimes.
> But thou base man first prostituted hast
> Our spotless knowledge and the studies chast.
> Apostatizing from our Arts and us,
> To turn the Chronicler to Spartacus.   (63-74)

Phrases such as the "wheel of Empire" and "though the World's disjointed Axel crack" are reminiscent of those images in "The Definition of Love" which also denote the destruction of an ideal state: "Loves whole World on us doth wheel" would be equivalent to the "wheel of Empire"; and it is destroyed by a "Convulsion" that would destroy the poles (or axis or "Axel") that maintain the ordered movement of an ideal love or an ideal government. This correspondence between the two poems, however, should also remind us that in the love poem, at least, the impulse to bring about a conjunction of the bodies was also felt. And, in these lines to Tom May, we are made fully conscious of the fact that "Vertues cause" is not only "forsaken" by all men; but, what is more important, it seems to run counter to the very forces of nature itself: "the World's disjointed Axel" is itself breaking up. Because in this poem Marvell is fully aware of the hopelessness of his cause as well as of the baseness of one who is forsaking that cause, it is possible to say that Marvell is quarreling with himself as well as with Tom May. But this point can be seen more clearly after an analysis of "An Horatian Ode."

II "An Horatian Ode"

When "An Horatian Ode upon Cromwel's Return from Ireland" was written in 1650, its readers were puzzled by the praise given to King Charles I. And readers ever since have been puzzled by Marvell's ability to deal with the burning issues of the Civil War without making his political position clear. The best known explanation is that offered by Margoliouth: "The ode is the utterance of a constitutional monarchist, whose sympathies have been with the King, but who yet believes more in men than in parties or principles, and whose hopes are fixed now on Cromwell, seeing in him both the civic ideal of a ruler without personal ambition, and the man of destiny moved by and yet himself driving (1.12) a power which is above justice (see 1.37)." But to understand the logic of the poem we must know how and why Marvell could place a mortal man above justice. Cleanth Brooks has argued that justice even in "An Horatian Ode" is on the side of the King: "the Right is no less right because it is helpless." But Douglas Bush questions whether Cromwell, "The force of angry Heavens flame," can be anything but totally good, since he is an agent of Providence.[3] More recent scholarship has emphasized the rhetorical tradition of the "Ode," the political situation in 1650, and the classical parallel of Cato's acceptance of Pompey which is described in Lucan's *Pharsalia*, an epic poem about the civil war between Caesar and Pompey. But even a rhetorical reading of the poem, which sees Cromwell as a Christian hero, concludes with a reminder that "no critic would want to explain away altogether the 'ambiguities' in Marvell's view of him." [4]

It is becoming increasingly clear that any good reading of the poem should take into account the ambiguity in Marvell's attitude. What is also being gradually accepted is that this ambiguity is not at all puzzling but is quite usual in any political situation. People in all eras have supported measures and men in direct opposition to their political beliefs and loyalties. For in such times what seems necessary—what *must* be done— takes precedence over what *ought* to be done. There is a disjunction between political ideals and political action. Such a situation confronted Marvell during the Civil War.

In 1650, Charles I had been executed; the Royalist forces had been thoroughly defeated by the Parliamentary armies; and Cromwell, having succeeded (on June 26) the more moderate Lord Fairfax as commander-in-chief of the army, was the dominant figure in England. But it is inaccurate to say that the English people or even a dominant section of them had created a republic. Few people had consciously desired to overthrow the monarchy. As with most great historical changes, events had built up their own momentum; the English people did not so much create as stumble into a commonwealth. Consequently, this government did not command a strong moral allegiance deeply ingrained in the people's minds through long centuries of tradition. It is in this sense then that most Englishmen of this period were monarchists in belief. If they were republicans in action, it was because the late monarch and his advisors had made serious errors which left no alternative. The Commonwealth was not the ideal government; it was only the one which the pressure of unusual events had made necessary. The difference between Charles I and Cromwell was, in this sense, a difference between a government which *ought* to exist and a government which men *must* support—in the absence of any other power capable of ruling England at that moment. It is this distinction between what men *ought* to do on an ideal plane and what men *must* do in the world of active political events that underlies "An Horatian Ode."

In the first part of the poem Cromwell is introduced as the "three-fork'd Lightning." We are reminded that " 'Tis Madness to resist or blame/The force of angry Heavens flame." In that world view held by Marvell's contemporaries (and well known by now to most readers of seventeenth-century literature), the heavens are silent, majestic, and stable. Lightning occurs only when there is something wrong, some departure from stability and order. It is a force of an "angry" heaven. Cromwell, therefore, is a force occasioned by some disturbance in the fixed, natural order of things. Like the lightning, he is hardly welcomed. This impression is strengthened in the next passage:

> And, if we would speak true,
> Much to the Man is due.
> Who, from his private Gardens, where
> He liv'd reserved and austere,
> As if his highest plot
> To plant the Bergamot,
> Could by industrious Valour climbe
> To ruine the great Work of Time,

> *And cast the Kingdome old*
> *Into another Mold.* (27-36)

Cromwell is industrious and valorous; but, like lightning destroying a tree, he *ruins* the state. The ideal order—the monarchy—is changed "Into another Mold." Any force which thus destroys a "great Work of Time," or a political system—which to Marvell seemed to inhere in the very nature of the divine order—was certainly not good or just. But, like the lightning, such a force is irresistible and *must* be accepted.

If it were a matter of the justice of the cause, of what *ought* to be, Charles would of course be preferred:

> *He nothing common did or mean*
> *Upon that memorable Scene:*
> *But with his keener Eye*
> *The Axes edge did try:*
> *Nor call'd the Gods with vulgar spight*
> *To vindicate his helpless Right,*
> *But bow'd his comely Head,*
> *Down as upon a Bed.* (57-64)

The "Right," even if "helpless," is on the side of Charles. But, and this is the point of the poem, we are not concerned with "Right" and "Justice," but with what *must* be done:

> *Though Justice against Fate complain,*
> *And plead the antient Rights in vain:*
> *But those do hold or break*
> *As Men are strong or weak.* (37-40)

Marvell thus parries the entire argument of the Royalists by granting it—and then declaring it irrelevant. The question of what is just is kept on an ideal plane of what ought to be, and this poem deals with the world of action, with what—at least to Marvell—must be.

We can now see the significance of the opening lines:

> *The forward Youth that would appear*
> *Must now forsake his Muses dear,*
> *Nor in the Shadows sing*

> *His Numbers languishing.*
> *'Tis time to leave the Books in dust,*
> *And oyl th' unused Armours rust:*
> *Removing from the Wall*
> *The Corslet of the Hall.*   (1-8)

In time of action there is nothing remarkable in a poet's forsaking his books; but that the books are left in dust implies a disjunction between the wisdom gained in contemplation and the sagacity needed in action. In action we need only to know what is powerful, not what is right. In the final section of the poem the amoral determinism is continued. Even the "helpless Right" is absent. Cromwell is a "Falcon," and "A *Caesar* . . . to *Gaul,*/To *Italy* an *Hannibal*"; all of these make a mockery of the claim that he is a "liberator." The "Ode" is, therefore, neither a grudging acknowledgment by a constitutional monarchist of Cromwell's greatness, nor is it, as Professor Brooks maintains, an impartial, dramatic treatment of the political struggle. The "Ode" is a skillful, highly effective argument in support of Cromwell. The diehard Royalists who continue to fight against Cromwell have only a "vulgar spight." It is this disjunction, therefore, between what *ought* to be and what *must* be that allows Marvell to praise King Charles and to support Cromwell without inconsistency.

But Marvell is not satisfied with proving that Cromwell is powerful; he is aware that he must also show that the power is good. And in showing this, he is not nearly so successful. The passage on Ireland is, of course, a grossly partisan description of Cromwell's campaign:

> *And now the* Irish *are asham'd*
> *To see themselves in one Year tam'd:*
> *So much one Man can do,*
> *That does both act and know.*
> *They can affirm his Praises best,*
> *And have, though overcome, confest*
> *How good he is, how just,*
> *And fit for highest Trust.*   (73-80)

What is even more significant, however, is that in this passage Marvell is admitting that the moral values cannot be ignored in the field of action. Cromwell, who throughout the poem is beyond good and evil, is, in this passage, "good" and "just." This inconsistency reveals Marvell's sense of the inadequacy of his separation between morality and action. He realized that he must not only prove Cromwell powerful but also just. To read the words "good" and "just" as synonyms for bravery and courage, as is sometimes done, is to beg the whole question. To show that the energy and power of Cromwell are equivalent to the "good" and the "just" is the problem and not the solution.

And the problem is not only political but one which involves the poetic structure as well. For about seventy-five lines Cromwell is praised for his invincible power. Only in line 79 is the goodness and justice of Cromwell mentioned; and strangely enough the Irish who were massacred by Cromwell are said to testify "How good he is, how just,/And fit for highest Trust." One critic has gone so far as to read these lines as intentionally ironic and therefore as a subtle attack on Cromwell. This reading is doubtful. But what cannot be disputed is that the idea of Cromwell being good and just is dropped just as quickly as it is introduced.

The next forty lines fail to mention goodness or justice. By dropping the idea of Cromwell's being good, the rhetoric of the poem is obviously weakened. For the reader tends to equate goodness with Charles as against the power of Cromwell. Consequently no sensitive reader, or no reader who can go beyond his own predilections, has read the poem solely as a eulogy of Cromwell. Some critics, it is true, have argued that the nobility of Charles makes the praise of Cromwell even more effective by granting the Royalists their strongest argument. This is quite true—up to a point. But at one point the poem does attempt to transfer goodness and justice to Cromwell. And the logic of the poem, as we have seen, does not allow this conclusion. The poet cannot take out of nature more than the energy and glory of "angry Heavens flame." There is nothing in his natural images to denote or connote goodness or justice. Marvell fails, therefore, in a purely rhetorical sense, to present Cromwell as one who "both acts and knows."

But that the poet tried to reconcile the "antient Rights" with the necessities of immediate action reveals that the second quarrel—that with himself—still continued. And although this quarrel within prevented Marvell from taking a clear-cut political position, his sensitivity to the claims of what must be done as well as what ought to be done allowed him to write a great poem.

III   Later Political Poems

The quarrel with himself can also be seen as the chief theme of two other poems which were written a few years later while Marvell was acting as a tutor to Lord Fairfax's daughter. To a much greater degree than in the love poems, the political poems reveal Marvell's inability to remain satisfied with the complete withdrawal into an ideal world. Whether because of a purely personal need for a patron—or because he had come to see a middle ground between the Royalists and the Republicans—Marvell, early in 1651, joined the household of Lord Fairfax. Since he was a tutor to the daughter of Lord Fairfax, the poems addressed to his patron are to a large extent conventional, complimentary verse.

But there is also something more in these poems. For in the retired general of the Parliamentary forces, in the man who had given up his power because he believed that the revolution had gone too far, Marvell felt that he had found a true leader. Fairfax, like Cromwell, was a man of action who "through adventrous War/Urged his active Star"; at the same time, like Charles, he had the right on his side. He seemed, therefore, to be the one most likely to fight "forsaken Vertues cause." Fairfax, however, did not fight after 1650; his retirement from the political scene was permanent. And Marvell was still confronted with an inactive justice and with a "helpless Right." Confronted with this dilemma, he attempts to join Lord Fairfax in a withdrawal from action; but, as we shall see in the next two poems, Marvell could not escape entirely from the political issues.

"Upon the Hill and Grove at Bill-borow" opens with an attempt to justify Fairfax by showing that even nature teaches self-sufficiency and retirement:

> See how the arched Earth does here
> Rise in a perfect Hemisphere!
> The stiffest Compass could not strike

> *A Line more circular and like;*
> *Nor softest Pensel draw a Brow*
> *So equal as this Hill does bow.*
> *It seems as for a Model laid,*
> *And that the World by it was made.* (1-8)

The significance which was attributed to the circle has been mentioned in previous chapters: the circle in the *Enneads* is a symbol of that which is self-sufficient and therefore perfect. The material body, which is only potential and lacks Authentic Existence, has straightforward motion, but the cosmic soul has circular motion. In the second stanza the idea of the moral superiority of the perfect circle (with its center equidistant from every point on the circumference) is made explicit:

> *Here learn ye Mountains more unjust,*
> *Which to abrupter greatness thrust,*
> *That do with your hook-shoulder'd height*
> *The Earth deform and Heaven fright,*
> *For whose excrescence ill design'd,*
> *Nature must a new Center find.* (9-14)

The word "unjust," applied to the mountains because they break the perfect circularity of the earth, works backward to the first stanza. It gives ethical force to such words as "equal," "Model," "Hemisphere," "circular," which, when first encountered, seem to be only objective descriptions of nature.

In the last two lines of this stanza we come upon a *non sequitur:* "Learn here those humble steps to tread,/Which to securer Glory lead." The "Hill," being circular, can be self-sufficient, secure, and humble; but there is nothing to indicate that it can attain "Glory." "Glory" connotes something which stands out from that which is level, equal, and humble. Marvell insists that retirement offers a "securer Glory" because Fairfax must counteract the glory which can be won in the field of political action.

In the third stanza the "Hill" is again praised for its retirement:

> *See then how courteous it ascends,*
> *And all the way it rises bends;*

> *Not for it self the height does gain,*
> *But only strives to raise the Plain.*   (21-24)

But the next two stanzas revert to grandeur and military prowess:

> *Yet thus it all the field commands,*
> *And in unenvy'd Greatness stands,*
> *Discerning further then the Cliff*
> *Of Heaven-daring* Teneriff.
> *How glad the weary Seamen hast*
> *When they salute it from the Mast!*
> *By Night the Northern Star their way*
> *Directs, and this no less by Day.*
>
> *Upon its crest this Mountain grave*
> *A Plump of aged Trees does wave.*
> *No hostile hand durst ere invade*
> *With impious Steel the sacred Shade.*
> *For something alwaies did appear*
> *Of the* great Masters *terrour there:*
> *And Men could hear his Armour still*
> *Ratling through all the Grove and Hill.*   (25-40)

The next few stanzas again praise the glories of peace, contentment, modesty, obscurity, and passivity:

> *Yet now no further strive to shoot,*
> *Contented if they fix their Root.*
> *Nor to the winds uncertain gust,*
> *Their prudent Heads too far instrust.*   (57-60)

But the ninth stanza reverts to Fairfax as the active warrior; we can see by the forcefulness of the imagery that it is the victorious general rather than the retired country gentleman who moves the poet most deeply:

> *Much other Groves, say they, then these*
> *And other Hills him once did please.*
> *Through Groves of Pikes he thunder'd then,*
> *And Mountains rais'd of dying Men.*
> *For all the* Civick Garlands *due*

> *To him our Branches are but few.*
> *Nor are our Trunks enow to bear*
> *The Trophees of one fertile Year.*   (65-72)

Marvell's difficulty is now clear. He shifts back and forth from action to retirement because he is not really satisfied with Fairfax's withdrawal from the conflict; and, at the same time, he is unwilling to engage in direct criticism of Fairfax's decision: "Therefore to your obscurer Seats/From his own Brightness he retreats." Unable to reconcile the desire for security with the desire for action and glory, Marvell presents contradictory attitudes which are not fused into ambivalent images. Instead of a development and reconciliation of the conflict, there is merely a shift in attitude from one stanza to another.

The same difficulty on a larger scale is apparent in "Upon Appleton House." We are not certain of the date for this poem, but the situation is the same as in the Bill-borow poem. Marvell's political sympathies are with Fairfax: his political hopes are entirely dependent on the leadership of a great man who has retired from the conflict. He can understand the virtues of contemplation and of action, but he cannot resolve the conflict between them.

Again, Fairfax's retirement from the Civil War is identified with the limited, orderly nature of his residence: "But all things are composed here/Like Nature, orderly and near." The greatness of Fairfax, however, cannot be completely circumscribed by this present existence. Men in succeeding ages will smile that he "Within such dwarfish Confines went." The poem goes on in line 89 to describe the history of an earlier Fairfax and his wife, Isabel Thwates. It has no apparent connection to the remainder of the poem. Yet in this remote story we can see Marvell's impatience with Fairfax's retirement from the world. For Marvell is not only satirizing convents, which is hardly remarkable in this period, but he is attacking the whole idea of a withdrawal from action:

> *Within this holy leisure we*
> *Live innocently as you see.*
> *These Walls restrain the World without,*
> *But hedge our Liberty about.*
> *These Bars inclose that wider Den*

> *Of those wild Creatures, called Men.*
> *The Cloyster outward shuts its Gates,*
> *And, from us, locks on them the Grates.*   (97-104)

The hero represents the force and daring which breaks through the "gloomy Cloyster Gates" (89): "But, waving these aside like Flyes,/Young *Fairfax* through the Wall does rise." The "Houses Fate" is to produce not a man who with "a certain Grace does Bend" (59), but rather a man who:

> *Shall fight through all the* Universe;
> *And with successive Valour try*
> France, Poland, *either* Germany;
> *Till one, as long since prophecy'd,*
> *His horse through conquer'd* Britain *ride?*   (242-46)

The emphasis on the active as against the contemplative life becomes even more explicit in the next section. The garden— the traditional symbol in Marvell of the passive, contemplative life—becomes a scene of martial activity:

> *See how the Flow'rs as at* Parade,
> *Under their* Colours *stand displaid:*
> *Each* Regiment *in order grows,*
> *That of the Tulip Pinke and Rose.*   (309-12)

Although ingenious enough, these stanzas seem affected until we see just what Marvell is getting at: the garden becomes all of England; and, since good is struggling against evil in the Civil War, it is also the Garden of Eden:

> *Oh Thou, that dear and happy Isle*
> *The Garden of the World ere while,*
> *Thou* Paradise *of four Seas,*
> *Which* Heaven *planted us to please,*
> *But, to exclude the World, did guard*
> *With watry if not flaming Sword;*
> *What luckless Apple did we tast,*
> *To make us Mortal, and The Wast?*   (321-28)

A few lines further Fairfax is urged to leave his retirement and enter the battlefield:

[86]

> And yet their walks one on the Sod
> Who, had it pleased him and God,
> Might once have made our Gardens spring
> Fresh as his own and flourishing.   (345-49)

This is as far as the poet can go in criticizing the retirement of his patron. But what Marvell cannot say directly he says indirectly. The description of the meadows and the mowers, as in other poems, is made to express very specific ideas and feelings. The grass becomes flesh, and the mowers are warriors:

> With whistling Sithe, and Elbow strong,
> These Massacre the Grass along:
> While one, unknowing, carves the Rail,
> Whose yet unfeather'd Quils her fail.
> The Edge all bloody from its Breast
> He draws, and does his stroke detest;
> Fearing the Flesh untimely mow'd
> To him a Fate as black forebode.   (393-400)

Even the simple pastoral scene represents the Civil War. And there is no escape from the conflict. Like the "Unhappy Birds," a man cannot be immune from strife:

> Unhappy Birds! what does it boot
> To build below the Grasses Root;
> When Lowness is unsafe as Hight,
> And Chance o'retakes what scapeth spight?
> And now your Orphan Parents Call
> Sounds your untimely Funeral.
> Death-Trumpets creak in such a Note,
> And 'tis the Sourdine in their Throat.   (409-16)

> Or sooner hatch or higher build:
> The Mower now commands the Field;
> In whose new Traverse seemeth wrought
> A Camp of Battail newly fought:
> Where, as the Meads with Hay, the Plain
> Lyes quilted ore with Bodies slain:
> The Women that with forks it fling,
> Do represent the Pillaging.   (417-24)

Just as the mowing and the gathering of the hay results in a "levell'd space," so the Civil War threatens to bring about a leveling of all men. The political references in these two stanzas are obvious:

> *This* Scene *again withdrawing brings*
> *A new and empty Face of things;*
> *A levell'd space, as smooth and plain,*
> *As Clothes for* Lilly *strecht to stain.*
> *The World when first created sure*
> *Was such a Table rase and pure.*
> *Or rather such is the* Toril
> *Ere the Bulls enter at Madril.*   (441-48)

> *For to this naked equal Flat,*
> *Which* Levellers *take Pattern at,*
> *The Villagers in common chase*
> *Their Cattle, which it closer rase;*
> *And what below the Sith increast*
> *Is pincht yet nearer by the Beast.*
> *Such, in the painted World, appear'd*
> Davenant *with th' Universal Heard.*   (449-56)

When the world order is being overthrown and the one man who could restore order, "had it pleased him and *God*," has retired, there is nothing for the poet to do but "Take Sanctuary in the Wood." Here the political implications of this poem unite with the religious symbolism (which has already been described in the appropriate chapter):

> *But I, retiring from the Flood,*
> *Take Sanctuary in the Wood;*
> *And, while it lasts, my self imbark*
> *In this yet green, yet growing Ark;*
> *Where the first Carpenter might best*
> *Fit Timber for his Keel have Prest.*
> *And where all Creatures might have shares,*
> *Although in Armies, not in Paires.*   (481-88)

If God wishes to destroy the world, the virtuous men have no choice but to find some means of survival. The woods serve as an ark that gradually becomes a temple:

> *The arching Boughs unite between*
> *The Columnes of the Temple green;*
> *And underneath the winged Quires*
> *Echo about their tuned Fires.* (509-12)

In this idyllic retreat far from the political wars, the poet gains a new perspective into the reasons for the catastrophe that has overtaken the country. By observing the hewel, or green woodpecker, as it destroys the oak, the poet is reminded of the execution of Charles I:

> *Who could have thought the* tallest Oak
> *Could fall by such a* feeble Strok'l
> *Nor would it, had the Tree not fed*
> A Traitor-worm, *within it bred.*
> *As first our* Flesh *corrupt within*
> *Tempts impotent and bashful* Sin.
> *And yet that Worm triumphs not long.*
> *But serves to feed the* Hewels young.
> *While the Oake seems to fall content,*
> *Viewing the Treason's Punishment.* (551-60)

If the regicides are as inevitable in a corrupt state as a worm in an oak tree or as sin in fallen man, there is nothing to do but to retire from the world. The retirement has already been described, in the chapter on religious poetry, as following a Hermetic account of the soul's return to a pristine state. In that state the withdrawal from action carries the poet into wondrous life (similar to that described in "The Garden") in which the most intense action can be enjoyed without any sin because it is transformed into a contemplative state.

But, as in "The Garden," the mystical state depicted in "Upon Appleton House" is described by a person who feels just as strongly the claims of the real world. One critic has commented on this paradox by noting that the desire to "escape from the anxious world of men, politics, ambition, love . . . indicates how painful and serious was this world's impact on Marvell." [5] Perhaps the intensity that the poet could not achieve in action (at this period in his life) is being transferred to the contemplative life. We can thus see in "Upon Appleton House" the same conflict, but in reverse, that we saw in "An Horatian Ode."

In everyday life, however, the transfer could not be carried out so easily. At least Marvell the man, as distinct from the poet, was not satisfied with the contemplative life portrayed in his poem. As we know from John Milton's letter, Marvell tried in 1652 to obtain a position in Cromwell's government. The erstwhile Royalist had come to support Cromwell, not only on the plane of action and under the impetus of necessity, but also, if we are to judge by his subsequent poetry, on the moral plane as well. The quarrel with himself, the conflict between his desire for the ideal state or leader and the desire to participate actively in the world had now ended. In the two famous poems to Cromwell in 1655 and 1658, Marvell had no doubt that Cromwell was good as well as inevitably victorious, and that the true justice was being brought from the contemplative state into the world of political action.

Marvell's quarrel remained only with those who still opposed Cromwell, and out of it he produced excellent rhetorical pieces, but little genuine poetry. For the rest of his life, from approximately 1654 to his death in 1678, Marvell was actively engaged in the world of politics, and the ensuing interpretation of his verse and prose becomes at the same time an attempt to understand and evaluate his political actions.

CHAPTER 5

Politics and Rhetoric

FROM 1654 until his death in 1678, Marvell's literary work was so directly connected with his political career that some mention must be made of it before attempting an interpretation of his poems. As was mentioned earlier, Marvell was recommended for the position of Assistant Latin Secretary early in 1652 by John Milton. The letter was addressed to John Bradshaw, Lord-President of the Council of State; and in it Milton recommended Marvell as a man "of singular desert for the State to make use of; who also offers himself, if there be any employment for him." [1] There was employment for him, but not in the government. He became a tutor to William Dutton, a ward of Oliver Cromwell. Marvell was now part of the official family; he wrote a letter to Cromwell concerning his ward; a letter to Milton concerning a political task; and finally, in 1657, he received an appointment as Assistant Latin Secretary. During the same period almost all of Marvell's poetry was devoted to celebrating and supporting Cromwell and the Commonwealth government. The two sides of Marvell's life are so connected that it is difficult not to feel that the criticism made by Marvell of Tom May in 1649 would apply equally well to Marvell himself: "Most servil' wit, and Mercenary Pen."

The commentators on Marvell have, however, been uniform in interpreting his political career in a more favorable light. These interpretations will be referred to when all of his work has been discussed. But some explanation of his political views at this point is necessary if only to see some consistency between "An Horatian Ode," "Upon Appleton House," and the official poems praising Cromwell. Even if we think of Marvell as a "Mercenary Pen" in these poems, it cannot be denied that the poet is the same man who praised Charles I and Lord Fairfax, as well as the man whose greatest poetry celebrates the withdrawal from the world into a mystic state of spiritual activity.

One of the difficulties that we encounter in trying to absolve Marvell from the charge of being an opportunist is caused by labels such as *Puritan, Anglican, Monarchist, Republican,* and *Independent.* Once these terms are accepted as fixed categories, it becomes impossible to fit Marvell into any of them for any length of time, despite the ingenious efforts of critics to prove that their subject is "really" what they themselves would have been. It might be simpler and ultimately less confusing if we were to concede that Marvell was an opportunist in the sense that he shifted his political position whenever he felt it necessary to do so to secure the kind of government he wanted. Instead of regarding the Anglican, Presbyterian, and Non-Conformist churches, as well as the Royalist and Independent parties as ends in themselves to which one should have lasting loyalties, Marvell regarded them as institutions which existed only to serve greater ends: religion and civil order. Since they are not ends in themselves, churches and parties should be supported only to the extent that they helped to bring about that mixture of order and freedom that Marvell and *most* of his conservative countrymen wanted.

The word "most" is not used here in an exact sense, but only as a reminder that most of the Englishmen who made any determined effort to affect the political climate during the second half of the seventeenth century were conservative in that they wanted (and ultimately achieved) the kind of government and church which conserved the Monarchist and Protestant traditions of England and at the same time allowed for those changes necessary to meet the new economic and social conditions. More specifically, Marvell and most of his countrymen were conservative in not wanting the monarch to become more autocratic than the Tudors, nor did they want a radical change toward a republic. In religion, they wanted neither a return to Catholicism nor a thorough reformation; they desired neither a strictly enforced Anglicanism, as had been envisaged by Archbishop Laud, nor such a large freedom of religion that the church would be disestablished. Above all, Marvell wanted stability and order. He was consistent, therefore, not in his support of any individual, or party, or church doctrine, but in his loyalty to the principle of stability and order which can best be termed "conservatism." He was an "enlightened" conservative in that he would accept those changes that were absolutely necessary in order to maintain stability and peace.

I *"The Character of Holland"*

Given these political principles, it is not surprising to find that the ideas and attitudes expressed in Marvell's official poems are conventional. Since these poems are written by a poet of great skill, some of the lines are clever, the metaphors are often striking, and the rhymes quite ingenious. If Marvell was paid for what he wrote, as his enemies declared and as it would be hard to deny, there is no doubt that he earned the money. But in at least one poem, "The First Anniversary of the Government under O.C.," we can still detect the same conflict with himself that provided the basis for his best lyric poetry. But before discussing this poem we will first mention one which is pure rhetoric, "The Character of Holland."

This poem is so conventional in its attitude and its execution that it was at one time ascribed to Edmund Waller. Only external evidence indicates its true authorship, for there are few of Marvell's distinctive qualities present. Not that invective and sarcasm are foreign to Marvell, as will be seen in the later discussion of the satiric works, but the invective in this poem is not lightened by any wit. We plod along from one weary couplet to another.

During 1652 and 1653 the Dutch fleet was engaged in a series of encounters with the English fleet. "The Character of Holland" was probably written soon after the battle of Portland (February 18, 1653) which, although the outcome was not decisive, was considered a victory by the English. Perhaps the lack of a clear-cut victory explains the lack of focus in the poem. At any rate there is little evidence of a triumphal mood.

The first two-thirds of the poem is devoted to a series of variations on the fact that Holland is below sea level and requires dikes to keep out the sea. The idea of land being below the sea provides an obvious target for Marvell's sense of paradox:

> Holland, *that scarce deserves the name of* Land,
> *As but th' Off-scouring of the* Brittish Sand;
> *As so much Earth as was contributed*
> *By* English Pilots *when they heav'd the Lead;*
>
> . . . .
>
> *Glad then, as Miners that have found the Oar,*
> *They with mad labour fish'd the* Land *to* Shoar;
> *And div'd as desperately for each piece*
> *Of Earth, as if't had been of* Ambergreece;   (*1-4; 9-12*)

There are puns on Holland, whole land as against "*Half-anders,*" "pickled *Herring*" as against "pickled *Heeren,*" and one quite imaginative variation on the sea-land paradox: "The Fish oft-times the Burger dispossest,/And sat not as a Meat but as a Guest." In the final third of the poem about fifty lines are devoted to the battle between the two navies. The tone is cynical and superior; there is neither wit nor feeling. And instead of patriotism, we see mere boasting:

> *And now the* Hydra *of seaven Provinces*
> *Is strangled by our* Infant Hercules.
> *Their Tortoise wants its vainly stretched neck;*
> *Their Navy all our Conquest or our Wreck:*
> *Or, what is left, their* Carthage *overcome*
> *Would render fain unto our better* Rome.   (*137-42*)

II *"The First Anniversary . . ."*

Far different is the poem written about two years later, "The First Anniversary of the Government under O.C." In one sense Marvell was now, in 1655, more of a "Mercenary Pen" than ever. A victory over Holland could be celebrated by any Englishman; antagonism towards another country is unfortunately not confined to members of one party. But the celebration of Cromwell's dictatorship is directly tied up with Marvell's political career. As was mentioned earlier, less than two years after he wrote this poem, Marvell was appointed Assistant Latin Secretary.

Superficially, the poem is an extravagant defense of Cromwell and his government, and at one time this poem also was attributed to Waller. But if examined closely, the poem is undeniably Marvell's, aside from external evidence. For beneath the conventional praises of Cromwell there is clear evidence of the same conflict within Marvell's own attitude that was expressed in "An Horatian Ode." The intervening five years had brought about considerable change in England, and Marvell's own position had also changed. He was at this time a tutor of Cromwell's ward and a close associate of Milton and other Parliamentary leaders. But the desire for a perfect state founded on the "antient Rights" did not completely disappear. Marvell may have left the retirement of Appleton House and Lord Fairfax for the life of action with Cromwell, but he could not altogether forget his "feeble Hope."

What Marvell had done, or at least had tried to do with his ideal, was to convince himself that it was being actually brought down to earth by Cromwell. One way of convincing himself was to look at Cromwell not as he actually appeared but as Marvell wanted him to be. But Marvell could not remove himself completely from the actual world of necessity and evil. The result is a poem that is more than a rhetorical exercise; it reveals the poet's quarrel with himself.

In the love poems the simple images such as grass, flowers, mowing, tears, and wounds were important not so much for their concrete qualities as for what they signified. In somewhat the same way, the actual events of Cromwell's rule are treated in "The First Anniversary" not as historic events but as signifying an ideal state which, Marvell hoped, might soon come about. And to give these actual events that mythic quality, Marvell first transformed them into natural forces. Thus, from the very beginning of the poem, Cromwell is the sun and the actual events are drowned in the stream of time:

> *Like the vain Curlings of the Watry maze,*
> *Which in smooth streams a sinking Weight does raise;*
> *So Man, declining alwayes, disappears*
> *In the weak Circles of increasing Years;*
> *And his short Tumults of themselves Compose,*
> *While flowing Time above his Head does close.*
> Cromwell *alone with greater Vigour runs,*
> *(Sun-like) the Stages of succeeding Suns:*
> *And still the Day which he doth next restore,*
> *Is the just Wonder of the Day before.*

Cromwell *alone doth with new Lustre spring,*
And shines the Jewel of the yearly Ring. (*1-12*)

As one critic has pointed out, the first stanza introduces "the
dominant images of the poem." [2] The power of time is first
a stream which brings all of man's aspirations to a close. This
is true only of ordinary men, for an extraordinary man, like
the sun, renews himself each day and restore "the just Wonder
of the Day before." The real importance of this image, however, is made clear in the next eight lines. In the Ptolemaic
system which is used here, the sun revolves around the earth
more quickly than most of the other planets; therefore, it is
not in any sense above time. But neither is Cromwell. He es-
capes "the weak Circles of increasing Years," not by moving
into a world of contemplation, but by action. His action is so
vigorous that he will "make him [Time] run." Cromwell is made
to transcend the world of time and necessity not by withdrawal, as in "The Garden," but by heightened action analogous to that of the lovers in "To his Coy Mistress":

> *'Tis he the force of scattered Time contracts,*
> *And in one Year the work of Ages acts:*
> *While heavy Monarchs make a wide Return,*
> *Longer, and more Malignant then* Saturn:
> *And though they all* Platonique *years should raign,*
> *In the same Posture would be found again.*
> *Their earthy Projects under ground they lay,*
> *More slow and brittle then the* China *clay:* (*13-20*)

When Cromwell "the force of scattered Time contracts," he reminds one of the lovers who "roll" their strength and sweetness
into a "Ball" (or "Sun"); while the "heavy Monarchs," by their
refusal to act, are analogous to the virginity which is reduced
to dust. Like a vegetable love, the unused power of the kings
(or of Fairfax who might have restored the monarchy) lies
"under ground," "More slow and brittle then the *China* clay."
In both poems time is conquered, therefore, not by a withdrawal into a contemplative realm but by rolling or contract-
ing its energies into a heightened activity.

But it is quite obvious that kings do act; they wage wars
very much as Cromwell did. Marvell recognizes this fact, and

in the next twenty lines he tries to show that the wars of the legitimate monarchs are petty in scope and aim:

> *They fight by Others, but in Person wrong,*
> *And only are against their Subjects strong;*
> *Their other Wars seem but a feign'd contest,*
> *This Common Enemy is still opprest;*   (27-30)

By thus characterizing the kings as oppressors, a new note is introduced into the poem. Not only is Cromwell more forceful or active than the legitimate monarchs, but he is also just and good. It has already been pointed out that such a transition, from being an irresistible force to being in the right, was attempted briefly in "An Horatian Ode." But what Marvell could not quite accept five years before is presented in "The First Anniversary" with complete conviction. For now Cromwell is no longer merely the force whose vigorous action is irresistible; he is also the good and just man. This transition from natural force to human justice is accomplished with great ingenuity. Astronomy, mythology, and a play on words are all involved in the next passage. Since Cromwell is the sun, the most active of the stars, he can hear the music of the spheres:

> *While indefatigable* Cromwell *hyes,*
> *And cuts his way still nearer to the Skyes,*
> *Learning a Musique in the Region clear,*
> *To tune this lower to that higher Sphere.*   (45-48)

The connection between the harmony of heavenly music and political justice is reinforced by using the Greek myth of Amphion, whose lyre moved the stones into place and built the city of Thebes. And finally the musical analogy is carried into the very wording of the Parliamentary group which called Cromwell into power: the Instrument of Government: "Such was that wondrous Order and Consent,/When *Cromwell* tun'd the ruling Instrument."

Now that Cromwell is back on earth, trying to establish harmony amid the political chaos brought about by the Civil War, he is compared to an architect who must arrange, not stones, but "the Minds of stubborn Men" into a stable society. At the same time we can also notice that the exaggerated praise of Cromwell gives place to a sober, if not profound, interpretation of his actions. To prove that Cromwell is just and is bringing about the will of God on earth, Marvell must transform Cromwell into a symbol rather than a man. To prove that Cromwell is necessary, that he is bringing about some measure of stability, is much easier. For it could not be denied that the Protectorate did hold in some sort of equilibrium the diverse forces, ranging from Presbyterians to Adamites, Monarchists to Levellers:

> *The Common-wealth does through their Centers all*
> *Draw the Circumf'rence of the publique Wall;*
> *The crossest Spirits here do take their part,*
> *Fast'ning the Contignation which they thwart;*
> *And they, whose Nature leads them to divide,*
> *Uphold, this one, and that the other Side;*
> *But the most Equal still sustein the Height,*
> *And they as Pillars keep the Work upright;*
> *While the resistance of opposed Minds,*
> *The Fabrick as with Arches stronger binds,*
> *Which on the Basis of a Senate free,*
> *Knit by the Roofs Protecting weight agree.* (87-98)

Marvell again uses the circle to signify perfection and stability. The opposing forces—conservatives, liberals, reactionaries and radicals—are all kept from dominating the government by Cromwell's power. It would hardly be a paradox to say that the revolutionary Cromwell was at this time a conservative force. And Marvell does not have to leave the reality of the political scene to justify this view of Cromwell.

A few lines later, however, a curious change comes about. Evidently being absorbed in the real world of political action makes Marvell wish for a more ideal world. For he seems to forget that Cromwell has brought to earth the order of the heavenly spheres: Marvell expresses a hope that an ideal man would appear who represents both justice and power:

> *Hence oft I think, if in some happy Hour*
> *High Grace should meet in one with highest Pow'r,*
> *And then a seasonable People still*
> *Should bend to his, as he to Heavens will,*
> *What we might hope, what wonderful Effect*

> *From such a wish'd Conjuncture might reflect.*
> *Sure, the mysterious Work, where none withstand,*
> *Would forthwith finish under such a Hand:*
> *Fore-shortned Time its useless Course would stay,*
> *And soon precipitate the latest Day.*
> *But a thick Cloud about that Morning lyes,*
> *And intercepts the Beams of Mortal eyes,*
> *That 'tis the most which we determine can,*
> *If these the Times, then this must be the Man.* (131-44)

The very images used at the beginning of the poem to indicate Cromwell's superiority to ordinary men are now applied to the ideal ruler: "Fore-shortned Time its useless Course would stay,/And soon precipitate the latest Day" is merely a rewording of lines 9 and 10. But, just as the actual ruler has become the ideal ruler whom one can only hope for, so the ideal quickly becomes identified with the actual Cromwell: "If these the Times, then this must be the Man." The word "If" is surprising at this point. For, as Margoliouth has already noted, this whole passage (11. 105-25) "takes its colour from the apocalyptic prophecies of Dan. vii-viii, Rev. xii-xx, and Cromwell's government is greeted as a preparation for the final fulfilment of the *holy Oracles* (1. 108)" (252). Yet at the very height of this apocalyptic mood Marvell is still skeptical as to whether or not it is really Cromwell who is destined to usher in the New Jerusalem. And the argument which follows is based solely on the fact that any decisive action is better than good intentions that are not carried out. Even if we know "not where Heavens choice may light," a man of action "Girds yet his Sword, and ready stands to fight" (147-48), rather than allowing "good Designes still with their Authors lost" (1. 158).

In the remainder of the poem Marvell practices what he preaches. He continues to describe Cromwell as if "this must be the Man," forgetting whatever doubts he may have concerning "where Heavens choice may light." And, if Cromwell is indeed "the Man" who will usher in "the Kingdom blest of Peace and Love" (line 218), he can be compared to Elisha and Gideon, and his mother to a Saint. Thus the Biblical references which permeate the entire poem make sense, and are not merely ingenious ways of flattering Cromwell. That we can understand the use of these metaphors does not, of course, prove that they are poetically successful in a deeper sense. To understand what Marvell is doing does not automatically bring about an appreciation of the poem. But we should notice that Marvell is not giving up his hope for perfection; rather he is trying to force the reality which confronted him in the actual world into the ideal perfection which until now he could only hope for.

In the next section of the poem Cromwell is not identified with natural forces; but, as in "An Horatian Ode," he is described as one who was brought into power by divine forces. Although inclined to remain obscure, Cromwell was by some "higher Force push'd" into power. A few lines later (265-78), a comparison is made between the ship of state in the midst of upheaval and a ship at sea in which "Some lusty Mate . . ./ The Helm does from the artless Steersman strain." And again, as in the earlier "Ode," King Charles I is seen as a helpless victim of a force greater than he could comprehend.

The final section of the poem is taken up with an attack on those radical (and reactionary) forces which were seeking to disturb the stability which Cromwell was imposing on England, and the poem concludes with effusive compliments to Cromwell from his foreign enemies. Marvell is very much at home in supporting Cromwell as a conservative force, and the lines are vigorous and direct. But, the more successful the rhetoric, the less poetry we find. There is some ingenuity however, particularly in the final couplet which brings us back to the opening image of troubled water:

> *While thou thy venerable Head dost raise*
> *As far above their Malice as my Praise.*
> *And as the* Angel *of our Commonweal,*
> *Troubling the Waters, yearly mak'st them Heal.*
> (399-402)

III   "On the Victory . . ."

Having thus overcome whatever doubts he had concerning the justice of Cromwell's dictatorship by appealing to the necessity for action, Marvell was free to devote himself entirely to rhetoric. And the poems celebrating a naval victory in 1657 and lamenting Cromwell's death in 1658 show little traces of that fundamental conflict which dominated Marvell's poetry in the first part of that decade. But the poet is never completely hidden from the official or semi-official apologist, and some continuity can be seen with the earlier poetry.

In 1657 (the year in which Marvell was appointed Assistant Latin Secretary), the English navy under Robert Blake won a great victory over the Spanish fleet off Tenerife, in the Canary Islands. The poem "On the Victory Obtained by Blake over the Spaniards . . ." is a conventional tribute to Blake, to the English fleet, and, above all, to Cromwell. After an attack on Spanish avarice (the ships were carrying gold), and a description of the paradisiacal nature of the tropical island, the poem follows the action of the battle. Returning from the New World laden with treasure, the Spanish fleet took refuge at the heavily guarded bay of Santa Cruz. Blake led the English ships directly into the harbor and destroyed the enemy ships without losing one of his own.

Although the thoughts and feelings of this poem are no more complex than the action, there is a continuity with Marvell's previous poetry. The most obvious connection is his use of paradox and the antithetical play on words:

> *Wealth which all others Avarice might cloy,*
> *But yet in them caus'd as much fear, as Joy.*
> . . . .
> *In thickest darkness they would choose to steer,*
> *So that such darkness might suppress their fear;*
> . . . .
> *The Thund'ring Cannon now begins the Fight,*
> *And though it be at Noon, creates a Night."*
> (*11-12; 21-22; 119-20*)

This play on words runs throughout the poem. But the effect is quite different from the word play in the earlier lyrics. In this poem the ingenuity in language has no counterpart in either the thought or the feeling, as it has in the lyric poetry; consequently, it calls attention to itself. The more interesting connection with the earlier poetry is the sense of distance and artificiality which we get even when the description seems to be so literal and objective. Just as the eyes, the tears, and even the name of the mistress had to be transformed into symbols, and just as Cromwell had to be made into an avenging angel, so this naval victory has to be made into some sort of fairy tale before Marvell could be at home with it. Even the horrible scene of men dying in battle is not allowed to disturb the enameled surface of the poem:

> Thousands of wayes, Thousands of men there dye,
> Some Ships are sunk, some blown up in the skie.
> Nature ne'r made Cedars so high aspire,
> As Oakes did then, Urg'd by the active fire.
> Which by quick powders force, so high was sent,
> That it return'd to its own Element.
> Torn Limbs some leagues into the Island fly,
> Whilst others lower, in the Sea do lye.   (127-34)

This sense of distance may account for the fact that the poet of solitude, ideal love, and mystic withdrawal should be so insensitive to the horror of the battle. Perhaps Marvell could accept and participate even vicariously in action only when its crudity and imperfection were removed. This tendency is carried even further in his final poem of this period, "A Poem upon the Death of O.C."

IV   "A Poem upon the Death of O.C."

The death of anyone is a natural opportunity to transform the imperfection which lies before us into perfection which we can imagine. For Marvell the task is too easy. For the transformation of the actual Cromwell into the saint whom we see in this poem is carried so far that Cromwell is hardly recognizable. Or, more accurately, Cromwell is recognizable only because of the historical facts and not because of his individual character. In "An Horatian Ode" and to some extent in "The First Anniversary," Cromwell's individuality comes through; even more important, its doing so brings about an individual response on the part of the poet. In this poem, the thoughts and the feelings (not the facts) might very well refer to almost any ruler. Although the facts refer to the death of Oliver Cromwell in 1658, the feeling may better represent the death of Marvell's hopes for an ideal ruler.

The poem opens by praising Cromwell's valor in war, his inclination toward peace, and the softness of a father's heart.

Almost fifty lines are spent describing the sympathy between the dying Cromwell and his daughter who died shortly before. The facts are accurate enough—Cromwell was very close to his daughter—but it can hardly be his fatherly qualities that made Cromwell what he was. It seems likely that it is the poet who finds the softness more congenial than the iron in Cromwell's heart. In line 100, the wider implications of the death are taken up. There is, conventionally enough, a sympathetic upheaval in the heavens and an auspicious date—September 3 being the date of many of his military victories. The connection with the heavens and fate is given a special twist by recalling how close Cromwell had been to death on the battlefield on this particular date: "Danger itself refusing to offend/ So loose an enemy, so fast a friend." That Cromwell is mourned as a symbol more than as a man is most evident in lines 227-28 where, despite some personal references, the real loss is that of "Valour, religion, friendship . . ." which "dy'd/ At once with him, and all that's good beside. . . ."

These lines are reminiscent of Donne's *Anniversary* poems in which the death of a young girl is used to signify a deeper and more general sense of loss. But unlike those elegies which are concerned with the meaning of death, Marvell is concerned solely with the body politic, not with man or the universe. When his poem does deal with the more traditional subject of death as a link between man and nature, the lines seem to lack vigor and freshness. Perhaps this lack of genuine feeling accounts for the fact that this poem contains a "very large number of borrowings from Vergil, particularly from the *Georgics*." [3]

But, if the conventional sentiments have little to do with the death of Cromwell, they do tell us something about the kind of man Marvell hoped to see as the ruler of England. And the grief may be interpreted as caused not so much by the death of Cromwell as by the death of the poet's hopes for an ideal ruler. It is not that Cromwell died but that, in the ideal sense, he never lived, which is at the root of the poet's grief. Perfection in the world of politics, as in the world of love, proved to be only a "Conjunction of the Mind,/And Opposition of the Stars."

From this point until his death almost twenty years later,

Marvell was to be concerned with the practical possibilities of the corrupt world here below rather than with the perfected world of his imagination. His satire in both verse and prose was to be completely concerned with actual events. And the quarrel with himself which had been the subject of so much of his lyric poetry now gave way completely to quarrels with others.

CHAPTER 6

Satire in Verse and Prose

THERE is no doubt that for the twentieth-century reader the value of the best lyrics is far greater than that of Marvell's satiric works. It is, therefore, understandable to find many critics and scholars lamenting the evolution of the lyric poet into the political versifier and pamphleteer. In more recent years an attempt has also been made to account for this change by relating it to the great shift in sensibility that occurred in the second half of the seventeenth century. Whether this shift in sensibility is connected to the scientific, political or religious changes, there is no doubt that the England in which Marvell spent his last twenty years was quite different from that which he had known as a young man. And no one would dispute the obvious fact that everyone is affected by his time.

But once this fact is granted, it becomes equally obvious that such references to history or to the spirit of the age tell us little about the life of an individual—and sometimes even less about his artistic development. For example, it is generally agreed that the lyric poems were written in the early 1650's during the Civil War. Yet these lyrics were concerned chiefly with love, innocence, sin, and death in both nature and man. Surely such poems as "To his Coy Mistress," "Damon the Mower," and "On a Drop of Dew" have no connection with Cromwell, Charles I, Laud, or Lilburne. Not that Marvell was unaware of the Civil War; his political poetry of this period shows how deeply involved he was. It is simply that, like all human beings, he had his own purely personal feelings. And just as it would be illogical to say that Marvell wrote a private poetry because of the Civil War, so it would be equally illogical to argue that he ceased to write such poetry because the Civil War had come to an end.

It would seem more likely that Marvell stopped writing lyric poetry and turned to satire for reasons connected with his own artistic development. As was shown in the first three chapters, most of the lyrics revealed a polarity between the desire for a perfection that went beyond anything offered by the actual world and an equally strong desire to participate actively in this corrupt world. This conflict reached its most intense expression in such poems as "The Garden" and "To his Coy Mistress" where both impulses seemed to be transformed, so that the passionate acceptance was linked to death, and the desire for perfect innocence was linked to sensuality. In a sense, therefore, we could say that the inward conflicts were developed about as far as they could go. Given Marvell's temperment and range of feeling, it is unlikely that any lyric poetry dealing with love, religion, or nature would ever go beyond what he had already accomplished. Perhaps we should be grateful that, instead of repeating himself, he did try a new path.

I *Satiric Poetry*

In the political poetry, however, a somewhat different development was traced. There we saw a gradual but unmistakable shift from a concern with the ideal world of perfect justice to a concern with the possibilities that could be acted upon in the real world. It was also pointed out that this change was part of a change in Marvell's own life from a classical tutor to an active participant in Cromwell's government. The need for action which was apparent in all aspects of his emotional life found an outlet only in politics. To take part in politics implies that the internal quarrel with oneself gives way to the quarrel with others. Marvell, therefore, went from political poetry to political rhetoric, to satire in verse and eventually to straight prose argument. Each step involves a more direct participation in the everyday world. Such an interpretation does not, of course, prove that the satire is better than the early lyrics; but it does suggest that the change in Marvell after the Restoration can be interpreted as part of his own development rather than as an unhappy accident of history.

Something more can be said at this point concerning the change from the rhetoric of the Cromwell poems to the satire of the Restoration. In theory, at least, Marvell could have continued after 1660 in the rhetorical manner. He could have praised the heroic qualities of men in his own poetry just as he praised Cromwell. If we compare "The First Anniversary" with "The Character of Holland," or more obviously, "An Horatian Ode" with "Fleckno," we find that Marvell's talent for praise is far greater than his talent for invective. Yet Marvell gives up rhetoric almost as completely as he gives up the lyric voice.

But this aspect of Marvell's development should not seem too surprising either. For even in "The First Anniversary" we saw the great effort that had to be made to forget the grim facts about the actual Cromwell in order to transform him into the ideal ruler. With the failure of the Commonwealth government, Marvell was no longer writing as an official spokesman for the party in power. Therefore his keen awareness of the imperfect reality, which had run like an undercurrent beneath the extravagant praise of Cromwell, could now come to the surface. If his achievement as a satirist is far below his achievement as a lyric poet, it is still true that the satire seems to come from the central core of Marvell's personality.

The most famous of the verse satires is "The Last Instructions to a Painter," written in 1667. Unlike the others, the authenticity of this satire is undisputed. Unfortunately for the reader, there are hundreds of references to the details of English Parliamentary history; in the Oxford edition, the notes come to twenty closely printed pages. It is possible, however, to follow the main outline of the poem by reminding ourselves of only the most important facts of Restoration history. The most important event for the understanding of the poem was the sinking of some British ships in the Thames by the Dutch fleet in June, 1667. Except for one heroic action (which is referred to in the poem), the defeat was a shock to the English. It should be mentioned, however, that its military consequences were minor, as a peace treaty with the Dutch was in the process of being signed. Clarendon, the Lord Chancellor, naturally was held responsible for the calamity. It should also be borne in mind that Clarendon's daughter, Ann Hyde, was married to the Duke of York (the brother of the King and the heir to the throne) under circumstances which created a great scandal. As a strong opponent of Clarendon and the

Court party, Marvell accepted all the malicious gossip about Clarendon, whether it had any basis in fact or not.

The poem opens with a plea to the painter to be prepared to forego delicacy and to concentrate on the kind of skill which arises from anger and indignation at the crimes which were being perpetrated in England at this time. This disavowal of skill in speech, and the claim that one's "Anger reacht that rage which past his Art," is of course an old trick on the part of the skilled rhetorician. But, against the background of Marvell's whole development, it is possible to see in these lines more than a conventional opening. For Marvell in this stage of his life does prove to be more concerned with his rage at the corruption and stupidity of the Restoration government than he is with art. Not that his skill deserts him; the ability to use antitheses, puns, and clever rhymes can be seen throughout the poem. But the devices are not used to create a new way of looking at Clarendon or at England; they are employed only to point up the conventional sense of outrage which Marvell shared with many of his countrymen.

Starting with Henry Jermyn, Earl of St. Albans, and continuing with Ann Hyde (the Duchess of York), the Countess of Castlemaine (the current mistress of the King), Sir Edward Turner (Speaker of the House), as well as the lesser known members of Parliament, the poet attacks them for sexual aberrations, greed, and general incompetence. It is sexual vice that, as might be expected, provokes the strongest lines. Completely removed from the ideal love which haunted the poet in his youth, the author treats sex now as simply a bestial act. "St. *Albans* full of soup and gold," is "The new *Courts* pattern, Stallion of the old" (29-30). Ann Hyde "nak'd, can *Archimedes* self put down./For an Experiment upon the *Crown.*/She perfected that Engine, oft assay'd,/How after Childbirth to renew a Maid."

After almost a hundred lines of such comment, the poem turns to the battle in Parliament over the excise tax. Marvell and his party were completely opposed to it, and the bias is not concealed. But the mock-heroic form allows him to achieve some distance from the party passions; as a result, the poem moves lightly along for about two hundred lines until the excise is defeated through the intervention of "A *Gross* of

English Gentry, nobly born,/Of clear *Estate,* and to no Faction sworn" (287-88).

After another sharp attack on the greed and corruption of the Lord Chancellor (the Earl of Clarendon), the sinking of the British ships in the Thames is taken up. Unable to pay the navy and unwilling to summon Parliament, Clarendon hoped to thwart the Dutch fleet by diplomacy and eventually by means of an army led by General Monk. "First, then he march'd our whole *Militia's* force, (As if, alas, we Ships or *Dutch* had Horse.)" (481-82). This strategy was of no avail, and Dutch Admiral "*Ruyter* the while, that had our Ocean curb'd,/Sail'd now among our Rivers undisturb'd" (523-24). The defeat of the English navy, whose great victory over the Spaniards Marvell had celebrated a decade earlier, causes genuine grief; the satiric tone gives way to a patriotic outburst.

This mood comes to its climax in the description of Douglas, who almost alone fought heroically against hopeless odds and, rather than surrender, chose to die in the burning ship:

> *That precious life he yet disdains to save,*
> *Or with known Art to try the gentle Wave.*
> *Much him the Honours of his ancient Race*
> *Inspire, nor would he his own deeds deface.*
> *And secret Joy, in his calm Soul does rise,*
> *That* Monk *looks on to see how* Douglas *dies.*
> *Like a glad Lover, the fierce Flames he meets,*
> *And tries his first embraces in their Sheets.*
> *His shape exact, which the bright flames infold,*
> *Like the Sun's Statue stands of burnish'd Gold.*
> (671-80)

That Marvell liked this passage is evidenced by his using many of the lines again in another poem on Douglas, "The Loyall Scot." But aside from its extravagance the passage is an interesting reminder of the earlier Marvell. For just as he had had to idealize Cromwell in order to accept him, so the grim reality of a man being burned is here transformed into some unearthly object. It is not enough to describe the simple heroic act, for Marvell is so overcome with the corruption of humanity that even the very flesh of the young man has to be purged of any natural qualities. In a preceding passage, for

example, Douglas is not only virtuous but almost totally removed from the sexuality that Marvell has by now completely
withdrawn from:

> Oft has he in chill Eske or Seine, by night,
> Harden'd and cool'd his Limbs, so soft, so white,
> Among the Reeds, to be espy'd by him,
> The Nymphs would rustle; he would forward swim.
> (655-58)

The consequence of this shameful defeat of the navy moves
the poem back to the satiric mood. Instead of getting to the
true cause of the inefficiency and corruption, the government
finds a scapegoat in Peter Pett, the Commissioner of the Navy:

> Whose Counsel first did this mad War beget?
> Who all Commands sold thro' the Navy? Pett.
> Who would not follow when the Dutch were bet?
> Who treated out the time at Bergen? Pett.
> (769-72)

But Marvell sees the real source of the defeat in the corruption of the leaders in Parliament, particularly the Lord Chancellor and the Speaker. The description of the latter is reminiscent of Dryden:

> Dear Painter, draw this Speaker to the foot:
> Where Pencil cannot, there my Pen shall do't;
> That may his Body, this his Mind explain.
> Paint him in Golden Gown, with Mace's Brain:
> Bright Hair, fair Face, obscure and dull of Head;
> Like Knife with Iv'ry haft, and edge of Lead.
> At Pray'rs, his Eyes turn up the Pious white,
> But all the while his Private-Bill's in sight.
> (863-70)

Immediately after this portrait, however, the tone changes
again, as Marvell describes the King waking up in the night to
see a vision of England whose "silent tears her secret anguish
speak" (897). This picture and the ghost of his murdered
father, Charles I, remind him of his neglected duty to his
country, and he decides to dismiss the Lord Chancellor. The

last section of the poem goes beyond historical facts, however, in suggesting that Charles was also able to see through and cut himself off from his mistress and other court favorites:

> *Through their feign'd speech their secret hearts he knew;*
> *To her own Husband,* Castlemain, *untrue.*
> *False to his Master* Bristol, Arlington,
> *And* Coventry, *falser than any one,*
> *Who to the Brother, Brother would betray;*
> *Nor therefore trusts himself to such as they.*

> (931-36)

For a complete understanding of the references, one must make use of Margoliouth's voluminous notes. But even a brief outline of the poem can make clear the sharp change in Marvell's political poetry. Although his tendency to idealize whatever he wished to admire still remains in the lines to Douglas, his chief interest is now on the grim reality before him. He is perceptive and shrewd about the real world; he knows exactly what he dislikes and, more important, just what he can expect even at the best. And this awareness of what is possible and probable makes him a keen political satirist just as he proved to be an effective politician.

But to write poems that can be read and enjoyed for centuries by all kinds of men requires something more. Among other things it requires an ability to make us see and feel in a way that we have not previously done. Great poems usually force us to get beyond conventional categories, as was done in Marvell's best lyrics. Even in satire, the best works of Pope and Swift do more than express what "oft was said." In Marvell's satiric verse, however, no fresh insight into corruption is given; neither Clarendon nor Castlemaine come out from the conventional categories in which they were found. What we can enjoy, however, in "The Last Instructions to a Painter" is the keen perception of an active participant who has not lost his skill in verse, even if he is no longer functioning as a poet in the best sense of that word.

The other satires have less interest for the contemporary reader, although their true authorship provides an interesting problem for the bibliographer and critic. Following the judgment of Margoliouth, it will be assumed that Marvell wrote the following satires: "Clarindon's House-Warming," "Further Advice to a Painter," "The Loyall Scot," "The Statue in Stocks-Market," "The Statue at Charing Cross," and "A Dialogue between the Two Horses." None of them is particularly readable; even as a group they do not reveal any artistic development which goes beyond "The Last Instructions to a Painter." But there is a wide range of mood and tone; and, even more important, they do reveal a political development which goes far beyond the official position taken by the members of Parliament.

In "Clarindon's House-Warming" Marvell is again at his favorite target, for the greed of the Lord Chancellor provides the basis of the satire. The poem opens by pointing out that the Lord Chancellor started to build his great mansion shortly before his country was to suffer an invasion (by the Dutch), a plague, and the Great Fire:

> *When* Clarindon *had discern'd beforehand,*
> *(As the Cause can eas'ly foretel the Effect)*
> *At once three Deluges threatning our Land;*
> *'Twas the season he thought to turn Architect.*
>
> *Us* Mars; *and* Apollo, *and* Vulcan *consume;*
> *While he the Betrayer of* England *and* Flander,
> *Like the King-fisher chuseth to build in the Broom,*
> *And nestles in flames like the Salamander.*
>
> (1-8)

The Lord Chancellor is then accused of obtaining the money from state funds, and the timber from "His Friends in the Navy [who] would not be ingrate,/To grudge him some Timber who fram'd them the War." Almost all the scandal is resurrected, most of it probably false, and thrown at Clarendon in the jingling quatrains. One reason, perhaps, for the light tone is that Marvell, as he was writing, was aware that Clarendon was already in disgrace.

But whatever victory was gained by the banishment of Clarendon was short-lived, at least from Marvell's point of view. "Further Advice to a Painter," written in 1671, is even more bitter about the corruption of Parliament than "The Last Instructions to a Painter." Turner is still the Speaker of the House, and together with "Circean Clifford" and "Pig-eyed Duncombe" they "devide the spoyls of England . . ." (22). But there is no longer a loyal bond of honest men, as in "The Last Instructions," to oppose the ruling clique. Even members of Marvell's own party have gone over to the ruling party in return for bribes. Perhaps Marvell's complete disgust at the political situation prevents him from standing back and seeing its ridiculous side. In any case there is no attempt to do much more in this poem than to show his contempt for the whole business.

In "The Loyall Scot," on the other hand, written at about the same time, the contemporary events are seen with greater detachment. The loyal Scot is Captain Douglas, the hero of 1667. As he enters the Elysian Glades, Marvell imagines that John Cleveland (a metaphysical poet who had died in 1658) is chosen to welcome him. Marvell's own conceits are seldom as extravagant as Cleveland's; to bring the two styles closer together, we are told that Cleveland had changed somewhat while in "Elisium." "Much had hee Cur'd the Humor of his vein:/Hee Judg'd more Clearly now and saw more plain." These lines might serve as a fair distinction between the two poets, except that the lines in praise of Douglas are hardly "plain" in any sense of that word. Some of the lines had already been used by Marvell in "The Last Instructions to a Painter." And in "The Loyall Scot" the grim reality of a man burning to death in battle is an idealized picture: "Like a glad lover the fierce Flames hee meets/And tries his first Imbraces in their sheets" (43-44).

The remainder of this poem is concerned with an attack on the bishops and with a plea for the union of England with Scotland. The latter subject is the occasion for some ingenious metaphors that are reminiscent of Marvell's earlier poetry:

> Prick down the point whoever has the Art
> Where Nature Scotland doth from England part.
> Anatomists may Sooner fix the Cells
> Where life resides or Understanding dwells:
> But this wee know, tho' that Exceed their skill,
> That whosoever separates them doth kill.
> What Ethick River is this Wondrous Tweed
> Whose one bank vertue, th'other vice doth breed?

Or what new perpendicular doth rise
Up from her Stream Continued to the Sky's,
That between us the Common Air shold bar
And split the Influence of Every star?   (75-86)

The references to anatomy, geometry, and astronomy hearken back to Donne and the metaphysical tradition; but the carefully balanced antitheses and the syntactical inversions suggest the neo-Classical style that was to dominate the poetry of this period and then reach its highest point in Pope.

A much lighter tone can be seen in the three satires on the equestrian statues of Charles II and his father. "The Statue in Stocks-Market" refers to the reigning King, and was originally made to represent the King of Poland. The poor resemblance provides the poet with an opportunity to attack the generosity of the donor, Sir Robert Viner, as well as the weaknesses in Charles II himself. It is surprising, the poet argues, that one whose fortunes were hurt by a recent act closing the exchequer should be so generous to the King who signed this bill. But the poor resemblance of the statue provides an explanation:

> *But now it appears from the first to the last*
> *To be all a revenge and a malice forecast,*
> *Upon the King's birthday to set up a thing*
> *That shews him a monster more like than a king.*
> (9-12)

The attack on the King is somewhat less direct, as would be appropriate to one who seemed at least to be a loyal, though somewhat critical, member of Parliament. The poet admits that the donor did make plans to have the statue removed for alterations, but he is skeptical of the improvements: "But alas! he will never arrive at his end,/For 'tis such a king as no chisel can mend." It is quite obvious that it was Charles II as well as the statue that was beyond reform. But the final verse modifies the criticism of Charles II with a note of loyalty born of resignation:

> *But with all his faults restore us our King,*
> *As ever you hope in December for Spring,*

[114]

> *For though the whole world cannot shew such another,*
> *Yet we'd better by far have him than his brother.*
>
> (57-60)

The poet's skill in using ambiguity is not lost; the reference to the statue in the first two lines changes almost imperceptibly to the King himself in the last two lines. This final verse is also significant as a clue to Marvell's political attitude. He seems at this point to be a loyal opponent of King Charles II, despite his keen perception of his corruption. What he seems to fear most is the Catholic Succession. But such an appraisal of his attitude will have to be modified if we accept as genuine the other satires.

"The Statue at Charing Cross," written at about the same time (1675), brings us back to an earlier period in Marvell's political career. This statue is of Charles I, the subject of the heroic lines in "An Horatian Ode." But the poem does not look back; it is concerned primarily with corruption of the 1670's. Only in the last stanza is there a hint of a more glorious past when the statue of the late King is warned not to face the palace:

> *So the Statue will up after all this delay,*
> *But to turn the face to Whitehall you must Shun;*
> *Tho of Brass, yet with grief it would melt him away,*
> *To behold every day such a Court, such a son.*
>
> (53-56)

In the final poem of this series, both statues come together. Written at the end of 1675, "A Dialogue between the Two Horses," contains a much more serious criticism of the government; so serious, in fact, that it would be difficult to reconcile the views expressed in it with Marvell's position as a loyal critic. The imaginary speakers are the two horses which form part of the equestrian statues. Not much effort is made to differentiate between the two voices. Both are equally uninhibited in the attack on Charles II, who makes both the "Church and state bow down to a whore," who steals the revenue, and betrays his country to secure "his own profitt and peace" (41; 57; 92). The boldness of these remarks is obvious to the poet, and one speaker warns the other that since truth is "many times being punisht for Treason,/Wee ought to be wary and Bridle our Tongue."

The anti-Monarchial viewpoint is even extended back to the 1640's. Charles I is given more dignity than his son, for he at one time "turn'd desperate Fighter" (as his son would never do) and died on the scaffold. But with all his bravery, he is still a "Scourge" who differed from his son in that he cut the throats of his people instead of "making whores of our wives and our Daughters" (132). Both voices also agree that Cromwell with all his faults was better than either king: "Tho' his Government did a Tyrants resemble,/Hee made England great and it's enemies tremble" (139-40). The conclusion is a plea for an armed rebellion:

> Yet the beasts of the field or the stones in the wall
> Will publish their faults and prophesy their fall.
> When they take from the people the freedome of words,
> They teach them the Sooner to fall to their Swords.
>
> (177-80)

How can such a rebellious feeling be reconciled with Marvell's official position as a loyal critic? One simple way of getting rid of this contradiction is to assume that this satire was written by another poet. And since all of these satires were published anonymously, such a supposition is quite possible. But the "Dialogue" is so similar in style to other satires dealing with the statues that Margoliouth is reasonably certain that the three "are by one author whom I believe to be Marvell, but definite proof is lacking" (310). The question of Marvell's political beliefs and political strategy brings us to the final phase of his work, the prose pamphlets. But before concluding the discussion of verse satires, some mention should be made of what was probably Marvell's last poem, "On Mr. Milton's Paradise Lost," prefixed to the 1674 edition of the great epic.

So immersed was Marvell in the contemporary scene that even the epic theme of man's disobedience and God's ways cannot prevent him from alluding to his quarrel with Dryden. But the allusion to Dryden's attempt to put Paradise Lost into rhymed couplets is not the only reason for including this poem among the satires. For the whole poem reveals the skepticism and the fears of a very practical man. There is a sharp contrast between the visionary sweep of the epic poem and the cautious distrust of the dedicatory verses. Marvell begins by "misdoubting his [Milton's] Intent"; he then fears the success of this daring project; and, in the third paragraph, he is afraid that "some less skilful hand" (Dryden's) will ruin the work.

Of course these cautious and crabbed remarks do serve, in one sense, to make the praise more effective. But even the praise, when it finally does come (after about twenty-five lines), reveals the great effort it took for Marvell to move out of the world of practical necessity into the visionary realm of the poem. To enter into the imaginary world created by Milton, Marvell had to go back to an image which he himself had used some twenty years ago. And strangely enough this image brings together Milton's poem and "The Garden":

> *And above humane flight dost soar aloft,*
> *With Plume so strong, so equal, and so soft.*
> *The* Bird *nam'd from that* Paradise *you sing*
> *So never Flags, but alwaies keeps on Wing.*   (37-40)

The lines recall the bird in Marvell's own Paradise who "whets and combs its silver Wings;/And till prepared for longer flight,/Waves in its Plumes the various Light." They also might remind us, by their contrast with the prosaic quality of the present poem, how far Marvell has traveled from his earlier state. He no longer wishes to soar "above human flight" but to devote his energies to the unweeded garden that confronted him in the England of 1674. Although a friend and admirer of Milton throughout the Restoration, Marvell's literary and political efforts took a different direction. He was less concerned with giving expression to his inmost feelings than with convincing his countrymen to take action on certain specific proposals. He therefore devoted his greatest efforts to his prose pamphlets, of which *The Rehearsall Transpros'd* (1672), and *An Account of the Growth of Popery and Arbitrary Government in England* (1677) are the most important.

II   *Prose Satires*

Although hardly read today, the first of these pamphlets was Marvell's chief claim to recognition during his lifetime and for more than a century afterwards. It must be remembered, of course, that his lyric poems had circulated only in manuscript and were not published until after his death; that, although his satires were published, they were anonymous; and that he rarely spoke in Parliament. *The Rehearsall Transpros'd* evidently made a great impression on his contemporaries. In the *History of His Own Times* (1724-34), Bishop Gilbert Burnet referred to Marvell as "the liveliest droll of his age, who writ on a burlesque strain . . . from the King down to the tradesman his books were read with great pleasure." [1] And a generation later Jonathan Swift expressed admiration for the satiric talents displayed in *The Rehearsall Transpros'd*.

As with so many satires, this work grew out of a long controversy and was an answer to a series of pamphlets by Samuel Parker, who was then Archdeacon of Canterbury and who later became Bishop of Oxford. In a series of four separate works (1670-1672), Parker had argued the case for strict conformity to the Established Church. The whole question of allowing freedom to the Non-Conformists had, of course, been argued since 1660; but it was not settled until 1688, with the accession of William and Mary. Charles II made many attempts to allow some freedom to all those—Catholics as well as Dissenters—who would not accept Anglicanism. Marvell and what eventually came to be called the Whig party also were in favor of toleration, but for different reasons.

Parker's chief argument in favor of not allowing freedom of worship was that the government or the supreme civil power had the right to determine what all men should do. He was sophisticated enough to recognize that legislation could not change a man's beliefs, but he argued that a man could keep his secret beliefs as long as he observed the outward forms. And observing the outward forms would help bring about "public peace and tranquility." As Birrell has pointed out, Parker's argument was very close to that of Thomas Hobbes, in that he was less interested in having men arrive at the truth than in preventing the factionalism which he felt would disrupt society.[2] Of course it is also apparent that, unlike Hobbes (whose doctrines were anathema to the Anglicans), Parker would have the church control the state rather than the state control the church.

[118]

This last point provides one of the best openings for Marvell's answer. He knew that the power of the church would be feared by the King and the Royalists for political reasons. Thus by attacking the bishops, Marvell could, in the words of one scholar, "further an alliance between the King and court and the former rebels." [3] In fact at one point Marvell goes back to the 1640's and tries to blame Archbishop Laud rather than Charles I for the Civil War.

The main argument offered is therefore a subtle one. Marvell does not in any way wish to impugn the authority of the chief magistrate, and he openly grants that the prince has the power to compel obedience in all things. But because the prince has the power does not mean that it is advisable to use it. Very tactfully Marvell argues that princes inherit "a generosity that runs in the blood above the allay of the rest of mankind" and are consequently disposed not to force people to go against their conscience. "A prince that goes to the top of his power is like him that goes to the top of his treasure." [4] This argument in favor of common sense actions rather than of dogmatic theories of state and church runs throughout the pamphlet.

Marvell even tries to make this policy retroactive in his famous comment on the Civil War:

Whether it were a War of Religion, or of Liberty, it is not worth the labour to enquire. Which-soever was at the top, the other was at the bottom; but upon considering all, I think the Cause was too good to have been fought for. Men ought to have trusted God; they ought and might have trusted the King with the whole matter. . . . For men may spare their pains where Nature is at work, and the world will not go the faster for our driving.[5]

Such a statement from a former Cromwellian is somewhat surprising, and some commentators have concluded that Marvell had changed his mind about the Good Old Cause. But if we examine the context of this statement, a simpler interpretation is possible. As a former Cromwellian, as a friend of Milton and supporter of the Non-Conformists, Marvell is in a difficult position in trying to ally himself with the royal power. For tactical reasons, therefore, as Dennis Davison points out "he had to profess loyal sentiments for the King, and execrate Cromwell and the Revolution." [6] One can go further and see in this statement a subtle defense of Cromwell. For immediately after this statement about trusting the King, Marvell concludes that what we can learn from "all the fatal consequences of the Rebellion" is that a wise prince would "avoid the causes." And the next sentence makes clear that the over-zealous churchmen (like Archbishop Laud and Marvell's later adversary, Samuel Parker) were the real cause of the unfortunate rebellion.

Such a reading of this passage would also enable us to reconcile the prose works with the very outspoken satires, particularly "A Dialogue between the Two Horses," in which Marvell calls for a rebellion against Charles II (such as actually occurred after Marvell's death). For one thing it must be realized that the sentiment expressed in the "Dialogue" was treasonous and that Marvell wanted to live. More important, Marvell wanted to be effective; that is, he was not willing, like Milton, to be forced out of the main currents of practical politics. As one scholar has pointed out, the prose pamphlets, in contrast to the verse satires, "state Marvell's considered judgment." [7] But the word "considered" does not have to be used, as in this instance, to mean "real." It may mean that Marvell's deeper feelings were expressed in the anonymous satires (and in a few personal letters), and that the "considered judgment" expressed in the pamphlets represents the modified opinions that were necessary in terms of the political possibilities that confronted Marvell. And one of the possibilities, as was previously mentioned, was to forge an alliance between Charles II (who had for his own reasons issued a Declaration of Indulgence in 1671) and the Non-Conformists. Of course, as all the scholars agree, Marvell was neither an admirer of Charles II nor a Non-Conformist. He was simply a Constitutional Monarchist and a liberal Anglican who was trying to use whatever forces he could to bring about the kind of government which England actually achieved after 1688.

Although its fame rests chiefly on its contribution to the political and religious controversy, *The Rehearsall Transpros'd* is also considered a landmark in the development of English prose satire. The title is taken from a play by George Villiers,

Duke of Buckingham, *The Rehearsall* (1671), in which John Dryden is satirized as Mr. Bayes. Marvell also used the name "Bayes" to designate Parker. Aside from the wit of the Restoration drama, critics have also noted (as did Dryden) Marvell's indebtedness to the controversial style of the Martin Marprelate tracts which appeared in the last part of the century. But the total effect of the pamphlet seems closer to Marvell's own time, and many similarities with Swift's work have been pointed out. According to Bradbrook and Thomas, the style of these pamphlets "pointed the way towards a more Augustan method of handling disputation." [8]

Parker replied to Marvell in *A Reproof to the Rehearsall Transpros'd* in 1672, and was answered in turn by *The Rehearsall Transpros'd: The Second Part* in 1673. Some idea of the violent and personal nature of the controversy can be seen by quoting the complete title of Marvell's answer. After the words "Second Part," the title continues: "Occasioned by Two Letters: The first printed by a nameless Author, Intitled A Reproof Etc. The Second Letter left for me at a Friends House, Dated Nov. 3, 1673. Subscribed J.G. and concluding with these words: If thou darest to Print or Publish any Lie or Libel against Doctor Parker, by the Eternal God I will cut thy Throat. Answered by Andrew Marvell."

With such a title we are not surprised to find that the invective is much stronger than the argument. Marvell begins by commenting on the intimate details of Parker's digestive system, goes on to his ancestry, his bad Latin, and his obsequiousness. The pamphlet does eventually come to the argument concerning toleration, but Marvell merely reiterates what he had already said in the first part of *The Rehearsall Transpros'd.*

Another attempt was made by Marvell to use his wit in a religious controversy. Taking his title from *The Man of Mode, or Sir Fopling Flutter,* a play by George Etherege, he wrote *Mr. Smirke or the Divine in Mode* in 1676. But this pamphlet is not nearly so successful as *The Rehearsall Transpros'd.* In the final year of his life, Marvell published an even less readable pamphlet, *Remarks upon a Late Disengenuous Discourse,* in which he attacks some recent attempts to deal with the problem of predestination. Marvell, not at home in theology, merely expresses his scorn at those who would try to deal with the dilemma of God's prescience and man's free will.[9]

As the decade wore on, it became evident to Marvell that nothing could prevent the Catholic Succession. He also realized that the attempt to bring together the King and the Non-Conformists on the common basis of toleration was impossible. It was the threat of Catholicism, therefore, rather than the absolutism of the Anglican Church that he addressed himself in *An Account of the Growth of Popery and Arbitrary Government in England*. Its anti-Catholicism and its support of the superiority of the English to "French slavery" and "Roman idolatry" are quite conventional. There is a detailed account of the treacherous actions of the King and his ministers in the Second Dutch War and in the long struggle in Parliament over raising money.

But to those whose primary interest is in Marvell, the chief interest in this long pamphlet is, as Birrell points out, the opening section. In it we find a vein of constitutional monarchy which is a fitting conclusion to Marvell's long struggle throughout his adult life to strike a balance between authority and freedom. In comparison to the kings of France and Spain, the King of England is a partner together with his subjects, rather than a tyrant:[10] "The very meanest commoner in England is represented in Parliament, and is a party to those laws by which the 'Prince' is sworn to govern himself and his people." Of course, in the light of Marvell's attitude towards Charles II, this sentence is ironic.

But if we recognize this passage as rhetoric, in the sense that this term was applied to the Cromwell poems, we can see that Marvell is talking about the kind of king he wanted to see on the throne. And in this pamphlet and in *The Rehearsall Transpros'd*, Marvell had to assume that Charles II was, at least potentially, the kind of ruler who could "govern himself" and who was subject to the same laws as his people. That Marvell knew better is obvious. It was another decade before the English people could find such a king. But without such an assumption all political activity would be meaningless; with such an assumption Marvell and his fellow Whigs, as they came to be called, could—even under the tyrannical rule of the Stuarts—prepare the road for a constitutional monarch.

But amidst all this serious activity the wit did not wholly disappear. *The Mock Speech from the Throne* is a short work, and it is not absolutely certain that Marvell wrote it. But most authorities believe it to be Marvell's, and from a literary point of view it is worth almost all the prose pamphlets. For the keen perception of the corruption of the Restoration government is combined with that good-natured ability to accept corruption as inherent in human beings. When the members of Parliament came to their desks on April 13, 1675, they found a speech which was supposedly written by the King, and which mocked the King's interminable attempts to get more money from Parliament. Even a short quotation can convey some of the flavor:

Some of you, perhaps, will think it dangerous to make me too rich; but I do not fear it; for I promise you faithfully, whatever you give me I will always want; and although in other things my word may be thought a slender authority, yet in that, you may rely upon me, I will never break it. . . . The nation hates you already for giving me too much, and I'll hate you too, if you do not give me more.[11]

From this speech, as well as from the verse satires, we get the impression that Marvell's serious preoccupations and genuine fears for the future of his country did not prevent him from enjoying the political struggle. His thinking was close to Milton's, whom he admired, but his temperament was not so different from the man he hated, John Dryden. As Edmund Gosse pointed out many years ago, Marvell ". . . reconciled the Puritan and the Cavalier as a man, and Republicanism and Monarchism as a public servant, because he was both and neither, but a personal third in which they melted in harmony." [12] Even if we conclude, with scholars, that Marvell's final position was republican, few would deny that he brought together some of the best qualities of the Cavaliers as well as of the Puritans. His political position had—like that of most of his fellow countrymen—undergone many changes since he had written "An Horatian Ode," but the equilibrium remained with him to the end.

CHAPTER 7

Marvell's Reputation

ABOUT two years after Marvell's death in 1678, a volume entitled *Miscellaneous Poems* was published by a woman who called herself Mary Marvell. The advertisement certified "that all these Poems, as also the other things in this book contained, are Printed according to the exact Copies of my late dear Husband, under his own Hand-Writing, being found since his death among his Papers, Witness my hand this 15th day of October, 1680. Mary Marvell." Since there was no record of Marvell's ever marrying, the relationship was always in doubt. In our own time it has been proved conclusively by C. E. Ward and F. S. Tupper (1938) that the woman who published the poems was Mary Palmer, Marvell's housekeeper, and that the claim of widowhood was made to gain some money that was held by Marvell at the time of his death.[1]

These poems seemed to have made as little impression on its audience as Mary Palmer's claim to be Marvell's widow made on the authorities. It took more than a century for any recognition, and more than two centuries passed before Marvell was accepted as an important lyric poet. The satiric poems did not fare much better. It is true that they were published frequently from 1689-1716 as part of the volume *Poems on Affairs of State;* but the texts were frequently altered for political reasons, as Margoliouth points out; and the authorship of each poem has never been verified.

Charles Lamb and William Hazlitt were among the earliest critics to comment favorably on Marvell's qualities. But to Wordsworth he was considered primarily a political figure who fought valiantly for freedom and integrity along with Algernon Sidney, James Harrington, "Young [Henry] Vane and others who called Milton friend." The line that follows, "These moralists could act and comprehend," may be an echo of one of Marvell's famous lines in "An Horatian Ode." But in any case, it seems likely that Marvell was better known as a "moralist" in politics than as a lyric poet until the twentieth century.

With the publication of Herbert Grierson's anthology of *Metaphysical Lyrics and Poems of the Seventeenth Century* in 1921, Marvell came to be seen not as a poet of nature (which was his usual classification in the nineteenth century) but as a poet of wit. Grierson ignored what he called the "descriptive poems" (except for "The Garden"), and emphasized " 'the metaphysical qualities'—passionate, paradoxical argument touched with humour and learned imagery . . . and above all the sudden soar of passion in bold and felicitous image . . . at once fantastic and passionate." [2] In the same year T. S. Eliot in his review of Grierson's volume attempted to place Marvell's wit in the main stream of English poetry. Instead of emphasizing the individual or the "metaphysical" qualities of the poetry, Eliot asserted that this kind of wit "involves probably a recognition, implicit in the impression of every experience of other experiences which are possible . . . which we find as clearly in the greatest as in poets like Marvell." [3] Grierson's emphasis on the distinguishing quality of Marvell "at once fantastic and passionate" proved to be the keynote of subsequent criticism of Marvell until quite recently. But through the efforts of scholars who have shown Marvell's affinities with older traditions of poetry and thought and through the efforts of some influential critics who find ambivalence in almost all good lyric poetry, Marvell's closeness to the "greatest poets" has also been apparent.

Mention of scholarship should begin with H. M. Margoliouth, whose edition of Marvell's poems and letters (1927, 1952) is still the standard and with Pierre Legouis, whose very detailed biography in 1928 cleared away all but the minor questions concerning Marvell's life. Legouis' interpretation of the poetry, however, is a different matter. Starting with the assumption that Romantic poetry was the standard against which Marvell should be judged, he sees him as "le précurseur de Wordsworth, de Shelley, et de Keats, le poète qui a observé le grive au rid su notes l'éclat de son oeil, qui a perçu le parfum des fleurs comme une musique surhumaine." [4] He therefore tends to apologize for "les bizarreries de son style," precisely those qualities which the readers of our time admire in him.

M. C. Bradbrook and M. G. Lloyd Thomas, on the contrary, tried to stress the metaphysical qualities and the ambivalence which were so admired by Grierson and Eliot. They also anticipated, to some degree, the efforts of later scholars to relate Marvell's poetry to the world view prevailing in his time.

Along with the conscious efforts of critics and scholars, there are other forces which affect a poet's reputation. The most obvious of these are the social and political tendencies which come to the fore from decade to decade. Fortunately (or, unfortunately, depending on one's viewpoint) Marvell's poetry—unlike that of Shelley or Dryden—cannot easily be identified with a political or social philosophy; consequently, it is usually liked or disliked for reasons entirely unconnected with the popularity of his ideas or philosophy. There is one notable exception, however. And, when we consider that Marvell devoted the greater part of his adult life to politics, it is perhaps fitting that one critic should attempt to judge his lyrics on the basis of the validity of their ideas and their feelings. In a long and sensitively written Introduction to *Andrew Marvell, Selected Poetry and Prose* Dennis Davison sees the Puritanism or moral seriousness as the dominating or at least triumphant theme of the lyric poetry, as against the Cavalier tradition in which some of the poems arise. For example, in "Daphnis and Chloe," he finds "a moral condemnation of the woman's conduct based on an aesthetic abhorrence of hasty lust"; and in another connection he states that Marvell is "nourished by the positive moral aspects of Puritan thought and feeling." [5]

Since Marvell (like Milton) is often taken over by critics with Anglican and Conservative sympathies, it is good to be reminded of his Puritan and republican side. But when the interpretation of the poems is made to fit a preconceived doctrine—whether Puritan or Anglican, ascetic or libidinous—the meaning cannot but be distorted. For the special value of poetry—and of all art—is that it can go beyond the fixed concepts into which we ordinarily, and necessarily, categorize our experiences. Whether we use Coleridge's theory about the artist's breaking up the categories to rebuild them with his secondary imagination, or some other theory, we can all agree that poetry does more than elaborate or restate, or even intensify, what we could say equally well in prose. And even if Marvell is not considered a great poet (and one must admit with V. Sackville-West that his range is limited), he is certainly a genuine poet in that his work has an intrinsic value and is not merely a useful vehicle to transmit some doctrine. As C. S. Lewis has phrased it in *An Experiment in Criticism,* we should "receive" a poet and not "use" him. To do so, we must be willing to suspend our belief about the doctrine, and to "seek an enlargement of our being . . . a temporary annihilation of the self." [6]

Marvell has been fortunate in that it is not very easy to force his poems into some preconceived philosophy or mood. For this reason, it is unlikely that he will cease to be read even when, as is inevitable, he ceases to be fashionable. Of course, "our being" can be enlarged in different ways. And at the present time it appears that what readers will find most interesting in Marvell is not so much the metaphysical wit which has already been absorbed into our poetic consciousness, nor a Puritan moral seriousness which is at best only peripheral to the dominant mood or tone. What readers in our time have found most interesting is Marvell's ability to endow his natural objects with symbolic meanings without losing that casual, almost negligent ease that we associate with the best Cavalier poetry. And this symbolic emphasis has been reinforced by the increased popularity of Yeats's poetry and, more recently, of Yeats's criticism. We are, therefore, more likely to enjoy the suggestive quality of the grass, the dew, the fauns, and even the lines and circles than did readers in the earlier part of this century. This belief in an animate living universe also serves to bring Marvell and Donne, despite their special qualities of wit, closer to Spenser and Milton, whose mythic qualities have also been pointed out by the more recent critics. [7]

It would be tempting to believe that the change in critical viewpoint from regarding Marvell as a nature poet, to a metaphysical wit, and then to a neo-Platonic symbolist represents progress. Perhaps we are now getting to the essence or the real meaning of Marvell. But strongly as any critic feels about the validity of his own interpretation, the history of criticism constantly (and embarrassingly) reminds us that the "real" meaning of a poet is a chimera. All that can be hoped for is that the interpretation offered in this study fulfills the need of the present-day readers to find in Marvell what is significant for this decade without, at the same time, losing the insights of their predecessors.

Notes and References

Chapter One

1. M. C. Bradbrook and M. G. Lloyd Thomas, *Andrew Marvell* (Cambridge, 1940), p. 41.
2. Rosemond Tuve, *Elizabethan and Metaphysical Imagery* (Chicago, 1946), p. 21.
3. John Dewey, *The Quest for Certainty* (New York, 1929), p. 255.
4. *An Essay on Man* (New Haven, 1945), p. 76.
5. *Image and Meaning* (Baltimore, 1960), p. 93.
6. This final line of "The Nymph complaining for the death of her Faun," it is true, suggests Christ rather than Sylvio. And the wider implications of the image should not be too sharply limited. But even if the faun is Christ, the reference is surely not to any aspect of Christ except his innocence. Thus Christ's death, serving as a reminder of man's original sin, can also be related to the death of innocence.
7. Pierre Legouis, *André Marvell* (London, 1928). ". . . l'image du fruit verte, ou, comme il dit bizarrement, de la 'fleur trop verte' évoque désagréablement pour nous des idees de débouche sénile; . . ." p. 72.

Chapter Two

1. *Andrew Marvell*, p. 69.
2. Herbert Butterfield, *The Origins of Modern Science, 1300-1800* (London, 1950), p. 16.
3. *Ibid.*, p. 8. For a comprehensive account of the importance of this image in seventeenth-century poetry, see M. H. Nicolson, *The Breaking of the Circle* (New York, 1960).
4. Bradbrook, p. 67.
5. Dennis Davison, *Andrew Marvell, Selected Poetry and Prose* (London, 1952), p. 44.
6. " 'Upon Appleton House' and the Universal History of Man," *English Studies*, XLII (December, 1961), 11, 10.
7. *Ibid.*, p. 11.

Chapter Three

1. Jowett translation, VII, 525. For this aspect of Plato's thought, see also R. Collingwood, *The Idea of Nature* (London, 1945), p. 76.

2. Edwin Arthur Burtt, *The Metaphysical Foundations of Modern Physical Science* (New York, 1925), p. 33.

3. *Enneads,* translated by Stephen MacKenna (Boston, 1949).

4. Catesby R. Talieferro, *Plato, The Timaeus and the Critias* (New York, 1945), p. 20.

5. B. A. G. Fuller, *The History of Greek Philosophy* (New York, 1938), p. 137.

6. Frederick L. Gwynne, *The Explicator,* XI (May, 1953).

7. Laurence Sasek, *The Explicator,* XIV (April, 1956).

8. Sermon XXVII, quoted in Robert P. T. Coffin and A. M. Witherspoon, *Seventeenth Century Prose and Poetry* (New York, 1946), p. 110.

9. Walter Pater, *Appreciations* (London, 1889, 1944), p. 18.

10. *Art as Experience* (New York, 1934), p. 19.

11. *Some Versions of Pastoral* (London, 1935), p. 136.

12. *Seventeenth Century Poetic* (Madison, 1950), p. 334.

13. "Andrew Marvell's 'The Garden': A Hermetic Poem," *English Studies,* XL (April, 1959), p. 6.

14. Wallerstein, see note 12: "And what is in neo-Platonic psychology the separation of the soul from the Divine Intelligence is, in Christian history, the Fall of Man and Original Sin," p. 352.

15. *Enneads,* see note 3, VI, 6, 8. Professor Røstvig finds another source in Hermetic writings. There also the soul and the spirit form intermediate stages between pure mind and pure matter. "The mind informs the soul, and the soul is connected with the body through the spirit, which in its turn is diffused and passes through the veins and arteries of the body." (See note 13, p. 8.) In respect to the attempt to find a chain linking mind and matter, there is no important difference in choosing one source or the other. But it seems clear from Røstvig's research that Marvell must have read Fairfax's commentary on Hermes.

Chapter Four

1. *Mythologies* (New York, 1959), p. 331.

2. Wallerstein, *Seventeenth Century Poetic,* p. 122.

3. For both viewpoints see *Sewanee Review,* LX (Summer, 1952), 366, and LXI, (Winter, 1953), 142.

4. John M. Wallace, "Marvell's Horatian Ode," *PMLA,* LXXVII (March, 1962), 44. For the resemblance to Lucan see also R. H. Syfret, "Marvell's 'Horatian Ode,'" *Review of English Studies,* XII

(May, 1961), 160-72. Syfret also finds that, although the poem is in favor of Cromwell, "in so far as there is a moral or emotional judgment made in the poem, it goes against Cromwell."

5. Davison, *Andrew Marvell, Selected Poetry and Prose,* p. 58.

Chapter Five

1. Augustine Birrell, *Andrew Marvell* (London, 1905), p. 50.

2. James F. Carens, "Andrew Marvell's Cromwell Poems," *Bucknell Review,* VIII (May, 1957), 57.

3. Bradbrook, p. 83.

Chapter Six

1. Quoted by Birrell, p. 152.

2. *Ibid.,* p. 160.

3. John S. Coolidge, "Martin Marprelate, Marvell, and *Decorum Personae* As A Satiric Theme," *PMLA,* LXXIV (December, 1959), 529.

4. A. B. Grosart, *The Complete Works in Verse and Prose of Andrew Marvell* (The Fuller Worthies' Library: Lancashire, 1875), III, 373.

5. *Ibid.,* pp.212-13.

6. *Andrew Marvell, Selected Poetry and Prose,* p. 238.

7. Dean Morgan Schmitter, *Andrew Marvell: Member from Hull,* (Ann Arbor, 1955), p. 258.

8. *Andrew Marvell,* p. 93.

9. According to Schmitter, the most recent specialist on Marvell's prose, this pamphlet is the "least interesting and the most difficult of all that Marvell wrote." Marvell seemed as hostile to theology as he was sympathetic to religious feeling.

10. Grosart, (see above), IV, 248-49.

11. The entire speech is reprinted in the above-mentioned books by Birrell, Bradbrook, and Davison.

12. *Andrew Marvell, 1621-1678, Tercentenary Tributes* (London, 1922), p. 109.

Chapter Seven

1. F. S. Tupper, "Mary Palmer, alias Mrs. Andrew Marvell," *PMLA,* LIII (June, 1938), 367-92.

2. *Metaphysical Lyrics and Poems of the Seventeenth Century* (Oxford, 1921), p. xviii.

3. *Selected Essays* (New York, 1950), p. 262.

4. *André Marvell, Poète, Puritain, Patriote, 1621-1678* (London, 1928), p. 171.

5. *Selected Poetry and Prose,* pp. 39, 43.

6. *An Experiment in Criticism,* (Cambridge, 1961), p. 137.

7. The influence of Cassirer's work on the mythic view of the world, already noted in Chapter One, is also relevant here. "It is not, therefore, in the least surprising that so-called myth and ritual criticism has become so powerful if so abused a method; since there is a very fundamental similarity (indeed a formal similarity) between Cassirer's mythical thought and the very structure of the literary verbal universe. . . ." Hazard Adams, "The Criteria of Criticism in Literature," *Journal of Aesthetics and Art Criticism,* XXI (Fall, 1962), 32.

Selected Bibliography

PRIMARY SOURCES

Editions of Marvell's Poems and Prose

Davison, Dennis, *Andrew Marvell, Selected Poetry and Prose*. London: George C. Harrap and Co., 1952. Contains most of the lyric poems and a good, if brief, selection of the satire in verse and prose. The introduction is an important critical work on Marvell's development.
Grosart, A. B. *The Complete Works in Verse and Prose of Andrew Marvell*. 4 vols. Lancashire: The Fuller Worthies' Library, 1872-1876. Still the only source of the complete prose works.
MacDonald, Hugh. *The Poems of Andrew Marvell*. London: Routledge and Kegan Paul, 1952. The best one-volume edition of the lyric and political poems. It does not contain the satires. The critical introduction emphasizes Marvell's political connections.
Margoliouth, H. M. *The Poems and Letters of Andrew Marvell*. 2 vols. London: Oxford University Press, 1927, 1952. The standard edition of the poetry, as well as of the letters. The textual apparatus and the notes comprise the basic sources for a student of Marvell.
Summers, Joseph H. *Marvell*. New York: Dell Publishing Co., 1961. Contains most of the lyric and political poems, a few satires but no prose. Modernized spelling and punctuation. An excellent critical introduction.

SECONDARY SOURCES

1. Longer Works of Biography and Criticism

Birrell, Augustine. *Andrew Marvell*. London: Macmillan Co., 1905. A good, brief biography.
Bradbrook, M. C. and M. G. Lloyd Thomas. *Andrew Marvell*. Cambridge: Cambridge University Press, 1940. An excellent brief discussion of Marvell's lyrics, satires, and political career, as well as an attempt to see him as a man of his time.

Legouis, Pierre. *André Marvell, Poète, Puritan, Patriote, 1621-1678*. London: Oxford University Press, 1928. A detailed, thoroughly documented biography and criticism. For additional comments see final chapter of this work.

Wallerstein, Ruth. *Seventeenth Century Poetic*. Madison: University of Wisconsin Press, 1950. A scholarly investigation of the intellectual background of Marvell's lyrics. Stresses the neo-Platonic and medieval sources.

2. Criticism of Individual Works and Shorter Essays

Allen, Don Cameron. *Image and Meaning*. Baltimore: Johns Hopkins University Press, 1960. Two chapters deal with the sources and meanings of "The Nymph complaining for the death of her Faun" and "Upon Appleton House." Referred to in the present work.

Brooks, Cleanth. "A Note on the Limits of 'History' and the Limits of 'Criticism,'" *Sewanee Review*, LXI (Winter, 1953), 199-222. Sees "An Horatian Ode" as a dramatic treatment of the subject and not as a praise of Cromwell.

Bush, Douglas. "Marvell's 'Horatian Ode,'" *Sewanee Review*, LX (Summer, 1952), 363-76. Answers Brooks's argument.

Carens, James F. "Andrew Marvell's Cromwell Poems," *Bucknell Review* (May, 1957), 41-70. Good analysis of the structure of "The First Anniversary of the Government under O.C."

Carroll, J. J. "The Sun and the Lovers in 'To his Coy Mistress,'" *Modern Language Notes* (January, 1959), 4-7. Explains the final image of the poem by comparing it to the phoenix, which dies in fire only to be reborn.

Colie, Rosalie L. "Marvell's *Bermudas* and the Puritan Paradise," *Renaissance News*, X (Summer, 1957), 75-79. Traces the historical and biographical sources of the poem by reference to Marvell's friendship with the Puritan, John Oxenbridge.

Coolidge, John S. "Martin Marprelate, Marvell, and *Decorum Personae* as a Satiric Theme," *PMLA*, LXXIV (December, 1959), 526-32. Reveals the similarity between the style of *The Rehearsall Transpros'd* and the Marprelate tracts.

Davison, Dennis. See above under Editions.

Eliot, T. S. "Andrew Marvell," *Selected Essays*. New York: Harcourt, Brace and Co., 1950. Places Marvell in the tradition of the poetry of wit.

Empson, William. "Marvell's Garden," *Some Versions of Pastoral*. London: Chatto and Windus, 1935. The first to point out the complexity of the images in this poem.

Foster, R. E. "A Tonal Study: Marvell, 'The Nymph complaining for the death of her Faun.'" *University of Kansas City Review*, XXIII (October, 1955), 73-78. Points out that the childlike diction and rhythm reinforce the pastoral quality of Marvell's poem.

Grierson, Herbert, J. C. "Introduction," *Metaphysical Lyrics and Poems of the Seventeenth Century*. London: Oxford University Press, 1921. Describes Marvell's metaphysical wit; the combination of learning and passion. A landmark in Marvell criticism.

Hyman, Lawrence W. "'Ideas' in Marvell's Lyric Poetry," *The History of Ideas Newsletter*, II, 2 (April, 1956), 29-31, "Marvell's Garden," *Journal of English Literary History*, 25, 1, (March, 1958), 13-22. "Politics and Poetry in Andrew Marvell," *PMLA*, LXXIII, 5, (December, 1958), 475-79. "Marvell's 'Coy Mistress' and Desperate Lover," *Modern Language Notes*, LXXV (January, 1960), 7-10. These articles are incorporated in the appropriate chapters of the present work.

Klonsky, Milton. "A Guide Through the 'Garden,'" *Sewanee Review*, LXVIII (Winter, 1950), 16-35. The first to reveal the Plotinian sources of the poem. (See Røstvig)

Mazzeo, Joseph, A. "Cromwell as Machiavellian Prince in Marvell's 'An Horatian Ode,'" *Journal of the History of Ideas*, XXI (January-March, 1960), 1-17. Argues that Cromwell, like Machiavelli's "Prince," must operate in a realm beyond our ordinary notions of justice.

Røstvig, Maren-Sofie. "Andrew Marvell's 'The Garden': A Hermetic Poem," *English Studies*, XL, 2 (April, 1959), 65-76. Also "'Upon Appleton House' and the Universal History of Man," XLII, 6 (December, 1961). Reveals by means of internal and external evidence the Hermetic sources of both poems.

Schmitter, Dean Morgan, *Andrew Marvell: Member From Hull*. Ann Arbor: University Microfilms, 1955. A detailed account of Marvell's prose pamphlets.

Syfret, R. H. "Marvell's 'Horatian Ode,'" *Review of English Studies*, XII (May, 1961), 160-72. Finds parallels with Lucan's *Pharsalia*, a history of the civil war between Caesar and Pompey.

Wallace, John M. "Marvell's *Horatian Ode*," *PMLA*, LXXVII (March, 1962), 33-45. Argues that the poem seen in its rhetorical tradition is a clear defense of Cromwell. (The essays by Cleanth Brooks, Douglas Bush, T. S. Eliot, and H. J. C. Grierson are reprinted in *Modern Essays in Criticism*, ed. by William Keast. New York: Oxford University Press, 1962).

3. Books on the Intellectual Background

The following works are all concerned, from different viewpoints, with the world view that Marvell inherited and which was gradually disappearing at the end of the seventeenth century.

Butterfield, Herbert. *The Origins of Modern Science*. London: G. Bell and Co., 1950. Emphasizes the gradualness of the change from a medieval to scientific conception of nature.

Cassirer, Ernst. *An Essay on Man*. New Haven: Yale University Press, 1945. A classic essay on the mythic view of the world.

Collingwood, R. G. *The Idea of Nature*. London: Oxford University Press, 1945. Reveals the Platonic source of the Renaissance conception of nature.

Dewey, John. *The Quest for Certainty*. New York: Minton Balch and Co., 1929. Shows the limitations of a symbolic view of the world in the light of modern science.

Langer, Susan K. *Philosophy in a New Key*. Cambridge, Mass.: Harvard University Press, 1942. Tries to relate symbolic ways of looking at the world to modern scientific thought.

Nicolson, Marjorie H. *The Breaking of the Circle*. New York: Columbia University Press, 1960. Shows how the world view changed from the beginning to the end of the seventeenth century by an examination of poetic imagery, particularly the circle.

Tuve, Rosemond. *Elizabethan and Metaphysical Imagery*. Chicago: Chicago University Press, 1946. Describes metaphysical imagery as being continuous with the Renaissance conception of poetry, and not a technique which was limited to a few poets.

Willey, Basil. *The Seventeenth Century Background*. London: Allen and Unwin, 1946. Reveals how the shifting conception of the world affected all the major writers of this period.

Index